T0125044

Unter schwingenden Dächern
Die Neue Messe Stuttgart

Beneath Sweeping Canopies
The New Stuttgart Trade Fair Centre

Unter schwingenden Dächern
Die Neue Messe Stuttgart

Beneath Sweeping Canopies
The New Stuttgart Trade Fair Centre

Herausgegeben von
Edited by

Falk Jaeger

avedition

Impressum
Imprint

Herausgeber, Autor / Editor, Author
Falk Jaeger, Berlin

Redaktion / Editorial supervision
Falk Jaeger, Berlin
Petra Kiedaisch, Stuttgart
Martina Fiess, Stuttgart

Übersetzung / Translation
Sean McLaughlin, Stuttgart

Grafikdesign / Graphic design
stapelberg&fritz, Stuttgart

Lithografie / Lithography
Repromayer, Reutlingen

Druck / Printing
Offizin Chr. Scheufele, Stuttgart

Produktion / Production
atio_druckkonzepte,
Leinfelden-Echterdingen

**Verlag und Vertrieb /
Publishing and Distribution**
avedition GmbH
Königsallee 57
D-71638 Ludwigsburg
T +49 71 41/1 47 73 91
kontakt@avedition.de
www.avedition.de

© 2007
avedition GmbH Ludwigsburg
und die Autoren / and the authors

ISBN 978-3-89986-091-7
Printed in Germany

**Bibliografische
Information der Deutschen
Nationalbibliothek**
Die Deutsche Nationalbiblio-
thek verzeichnet diese
Publikation in der Deutschen
Nationalbibliografie; detail-
lierte bibliografische Daten
sind im Internet über
http://dnb.d-nb.de abrufbar.

**Bibliographic information
published by the Deutsche
Nationalbibliothek**
The Deutsche Nationalbibliothek
lists this publication in the
Deutsche Nationalbibliografie;
detailed bibliographic data
are available in the Internet at
http://dnb.d-nb.de.

Inhalt

Contents

Foreword
Ulrich Bauer, Managing Director
Projektgesellschaft
Neue Messe GmbH & Co. KG

Vorwort
Ulrich Bauer, Geschäftsführer
Projektgesellschaft
Neue Messe GmbH & Co. KG

Wer im Bereich des Flughafens Stuttgart auf der Autobahn A 8 zwischen München und Karlsruhe unterwegs ist, unterquert eine gewaltige Stahlkonstruktion, die sich bogenförmig über die Autobahn spannt: das Parkhaus der Neuen Messe Stuttgart. Seine kühne Fachwerkstruktur mit über 400 Meter Länge macht es schon heute zum Wahrzeichen der Neuen Messe Stuttgart.

Die nunmehr fertiggestellte Messe hat eine lange und einzigartige Vorgeschichte. Bereits im Jahr 1993 wurde von den Verantwortlichen nach einem geeigneten Standort für eine neue Messe gesucht; das alte Gelände auf dem Killesberg war zu klein geworden. Es sollte eine internationale, überregionale Messe werden, die den hohen Anforderungen des AUMA (Ausstellungs- und Messe-Ausschuss der Deutschen Wirtschaft e.V.) genügt: mindestens 100.000 Quadratmeter Bruttohallenfläche, eine optimale logistische Anbindung der Messehallen und gleichzeitig eine gute Erreichbarkeit auf allen Verkehrswegen. Ein erster Suchlauf, bei dem mehrere Dutzend Standorte untersucht wurden, landete punktgenau auf einer Ackerfläche zwischen dem Flughafen Stuttgart und der Bundesautobahn A 8 auf dem Gebiet der Stadt Leinfelden-Echterdingen. Dieses Areal erfüllte zwar alle Voraussetzungen, stieß aber bei einem großen Teil der Bevölkerung, den Landwirten sowie dem Gemeinderat auf schärfsten Widerstand. Vielfältige Versuche, die Stadt wie auch betroffene Grundstückseigentümer von den positiven Impulsen der Messe zu überzeugen und mit einem attraktiven Preisangebot zum Verkauf zu bewegen, scheiterten zunächst.

Das Land Baden-Württemberg, die Landeshauptstadt Stuttgart und der Verband Region Stuttgart gründeten 1998 die Projektgesellschaft Neue Messe GmbH & Co.KG und entschieden sich trotz vieler Einwände für die Lage am Flughafen, da sie einmalig verkehrsgünstig ist. Dem Verband Region Stuttgart gebührt das Verdienst, sich über Jahre hinweg intensiv und erfolgreich für die regionalplanerische Sicherung des neuen Messeplatzes eingesetzt zu haben. Im Dezember 1998 wurde das Landesmessegesetz beschlossen, das die Grundlage für die Genehmigung im Rahmen eines Planfeststellungsverfahrens bildete.

Anyone driving past Stuttgart's international airport on the A8 motorway between Munich and Karlsruhe passes beneath a massive new steel construction arching completely over the motorway: the multi-storey car park of the new Stuttgart Trade Fair Centre. Its bold framework structure with a length or more than 400 meters destines it to become the emblem of the new Stuttgart Trade Fair Centre.

The lead-up to the completed trade fair centre was long and unique. The parties responsible started looking for a suitable location for the new trade fair as early as 1993 as the old site in Killesberg had become far too small. The aim was to create an international, interregional trade fair centre to meet the high requirements of AUMA (Ausstellungs- und Messe-Ausschuss der Deutschen Wirtschaft e.V.), a body of German industry for exhibitions and trade fairs: a gross hall area of at least 100,000 square metres, optimum logistical links between the individual exhibition halls and, at the same time, ease of access by road, rail or plane. An initial search, during which several dozen locations were investigated, finally focussed on a stretch of farmland between Stuttgart's airport and the A8 motorway in a municipal district of Leinfelden-Echterdingen. The choice satisfied all the requirements that had been specified in advance but was greeted with enormous resistance by local farmers, the district council and a large part of the population. Numerous attempts to convince the town and the affected landowners of the benefits the trade fair centre would bring met with failure, at least initially.

In 1998, the state of Baden-Württemberg, the state capital Stuttgart and the Verband Region Stuttgart (a political organisation with elected members representing and promoting the interests of the Stuttgart region) established a company with the name Projektgesellschaft Neue Messe GmbH & Co.KG and, in spite of the many objections, decided in favour of the site next to the airport due to its unique transport connections. The Verband Region Stuttgart deserves thanks for its intensive and successful dedication to ensuring that the choice of the new trade fair centre location was adopted in the plans for the region. In December 1998, the state trade fair law was passed, forming the basis for approval in the framework of the planning approval procedure.

Die Projektgesellschaft Neue Messe betrieb Planung, Grundstücks-beschaffung und Bau der Neuen Messe und lobte bereits im März 1999 einen internationalen, mehrstufigen Architektenwettbewerb aus. Ein hochkarätig besetztes Preisgericht entschied sich im Februar 2000 für den architektonisch und städtebaulich überzeugenden Entwurf der Architekten Wulf & Partner. Bei der weiteren Überarbeitung gelang es den Architekten, Fachingenieuren und Verkehrsplanern eine Messe zu gestalten, die neben den funktionalen Bedürf-nissen auch allen verkehrlichen, ökonomischen und ökologischen Anforderungen gerecht wird, ohne den ursprünglichen Entwurfsgedanken zu verwässern.

Eine architektonische Besonderheit des Wulf'schen Entwurfs sind die schwingenden Dächer der Hallen, die ähnlich einer Hängebrücke aus Zugbändern geformt sind. Begrünung wie Photovoltaik tragen zu einem hohen ökologischen Mehrwert bei, der den Intentionen der Auslobung entspricht. Die Parkhausfinger sind ebenfalls begrünt und stellen mit ihrer konvexen Form den Kontrapunkt zu den konkav hängenden Hallendächern dar. Neben dem Parkhaus mit seinen über 4000 Stellplätzen ist die Hochhalle das architektonische Highlight der Neuen Messe Stuttgart. Sie beeindruckt durch das attraktiv geformte, zirkuszelt-artige Dach und wirkt trotz ihrer Größe einladend. Der großzügig geplante Ein-gang Ost erschließt neben den Messehallen auch das südlich angrenzende ICS Internationales Congresscenter Stuttgart, das mit über 9000 Plätzen interna-tionalen Ansprüchen genügt.

Die Realisierung dieses gewaltigen Baus war mit einer Fülle von Widrigkei-ten und Hindernissen gepflastert. Dank der herausragenden Zusammenarbeit mit den Gesellschaftern Land Baden-Württemberg, Landeshauptstadt Stuttgart, Verband Region Stuttgart und Flughafen Stuttgart ist es der Projektgesellschaft Neue Messe gelungen, dieses große Werk zu planen, alle Genehmigungen zu erhal-ten und binnen dreier Jahre zu bauen.

Projektgesellschaft Neue Messe was responsible for planning, land procurement and construction of the new centre and, in March 1999, sent out invitations to participate in an international architectural competition made up of several phases. In February 2000, a jury composed of highly respected luminaries from the region decided in favour of a preliminary design by Wulf & Partner architects which was convincing in terms of its architectural and urban planning aspects. After refining the basic design, the architects, engineers and traffic planners succeeded in designing a trade fair centre which not only satisfied functional needs but also met econo-mic, ecological and transport-related requirements with-out any dilution of the original idea underlying the design.

The sweeping canopy-like roofs that cover the halls and are shaped like suspension bridges composed of beam ties are a special architectural feature of the design created by Wulf & Partner. Landscaped areas and photovoltaic systems contribute a high level of value added, corresponding to the original ecological intentions of the competition. The elongated sections of the multi-storey car park also have landscaped areas and, with their convex form, serve as a counterpoint to the con-cave hall roofs. Apart from the multi-storey car park, which has over 4000 parking spaces, the high hall is the architectural highlight of the new Stuttgart Trade Fair Centre. Its fascinatingly unusual roof in the form of a cir-cus tent is impressive and, in spite of its size, the build-ing radiates an inviting aura to observers. The spacious east entrance leads to the trade fair halls and also, on the south side, to the ICS International Congress Centre Stuttgart, which has 9,000 seats and thus meets inter-national requirements.

Completion of this enormous structure was ac-companied by a multitude of problems and obstacles. Yet, thanks to outstanding collaboration with the state of Baden-Württemberg, Stuttgart the state capital and the Verband Region Stuttgart, Projektgesellschaft Neue Messe succeeded in planning this huge project, ob-taining all the approvals and building it within just three years.

Eine grüne Mittelachse und begrünte
Dächer sind ein Charakteristikum der Messe

A green central axis and planted roofs are
a characterising feature of the trade fair centre

Die Rampenspindeln des Parkhauses entwickeln trotz
ihrer Dimensionen skulpturalen Charakter

The helical ramps of the multi-storey car park have a
sculptural character in spite of their dimensions

Marktplatz – Stadtgarten – Killesberg

Die Geschichte der Messe in Stuttgart beginnt nicht erst mit dem Cannstatter Volksfest

Market square – Municipal park – Killesberg

The history of the trade fair in Stuttgart does not begin with the annual amusement fair in Bad Canstatt.

Marktplatz – Stadtgarten – Killesberg

Die Geschichte der Messe in Stuttgart beginnt nicht erst mit dem Cannstatter Volksfest

Die Rolle, die Stuttgart heute im internationalen Messewesen einzunehmen sich anschickt, konnte die Stadt in früheren Jahrhunderten nicht für sich beanspruchen. Städte von überregionaler Bedeutung zeichneten sich als Typus durch differenzierte Wirtschaftsformen und einen eigenständigen rechtlichen Status der Handel und vorindustrielle Produktion betreibenden Bürger aus – und durch Handelsbeziehungen nach nah und fern, die Markt, Jahrmarkt und Messe mit sich brachten. Handelsstädte wie Frankfurt am Main oder Leipzig erhielten schon im ersten Kaiserreich 1240 bzw. 1268 Messeprivilegien.

Stuttgart lag abseits der Handelswege. »Die Demonstration der ›Stadt‹ lässt Jahrhunderte auf sich warten«, schreibt Otto Borst, im Grunde genommen bis ins frühe 19. Jahrhundert, als das dynastische Element seine das Gemeinwesen bestimmende Kraft verlor, als sich die Residenzstadt aus ökonomischen Gründen mit Straßen und Eisenbahnlinien in die überregionalen Verkehrsströme einklinkte und langsam aus der bleiernen Abhängigkeit von den Regenten löste.

Auch der andere Ursprung des Messewesens fand in Stuttgart keinen Wurzelgrund. Verkaufen und Vergnügen, Messe und Kirmes waren untrennbar verbunden. Wo viele Menschen zusammenkamen, die teilweise weit anreisten und für die Terminplanung noch nicht Stress im Stundentakt bedeutete, war Zeit und Bedarf für Unterhaltung jeglicher Art. Märkte und Messen mit überregionaler Strahlkraft wurden seit dem Mittelalter immer im Zusammenhang mit kirchlichen Anlässen und Festen abgehalten.

Market square – Municipal park – Killesberg

The history of the trade fair in Stuttgart does not begin with the annual amusement fair in Bad Canstatt.

The role that Stuttgart now intends to play as a venue for international trade fairs was impossible in the last few centuries. Cities of interregional importance were typified by their differentiated economic forms and by the independent legal status of their trading and pre-industrial production activities. They were also characterised by local and long-distance trading relations associated with their markets, fairgrounds and trade fair events. Trading cities such as Frankfurt am Main or Leipzig were awarded trade fair privileges in the first Reich in the years 1240 and 1268.

But Stuttgart was simply not located along the main trading routes. »It would be centuries before Stuttgart could justify its claim to be a city«, wrote historian Otto Borst. In fact, it took until the early 19th century when the dynastic element lost its power to determine the life of the community and, for economic reasons, the city – which was the royal seat at the time – linked up its roads and tramlines to interregional traffic routes and slowly detached itself from its leaden depency on the regents.

The other origin of the trade fair as an event was not reflected in the history of Stuttgart either. Trading and pleasure, trade fair and amusement fair used to be inseparably intertwined. Gatherings of people, some of whom came from far away and were not yet tied to the debilitating stress of today's tight time schedules, had time for and, in fact, needed entertainment of all kinds. From the Middle Ages onwards, markets and trade fairs attracting visitors from various regions were always conducted in conjunction with religious events and festivals.

It was not until the modern trade fair with fixed venues and the necessary infrastructure was developed in the 19th century that trade fairs were uncoupled from the religious calendar and its festivals. Religious gatherings were held in the village and kept their fairground aspect, hardly deviating from their original forms in the

Seite 018
Gewerbehalle mit Landesgewerbeausstellung
an der Kriegsbergstraße, erbaut 1881

Page 018
Hall of commerce with state industrial exhibition
in Kriegsbergstrasse, built 1881

Erst die Entwicklung des eigentlichen Messewesens im 19. Jahrhundert mit festen Standorten und der notwendigen Infrastruktur hat die Messen vom Kirchenkalender abgekoppelt. Die Kirchweih blieb im Dorf und behielt ihren Jahrmarkt, der sich von der mittelalterlichen Abkunft kaum entfernte. Die städtischen Feste wuchsen zum Rummel mit Bierzelt und Fahrbetrieben ohne Markt und Messe. Seitdem ist die Verbindung Volksfest und Messe abgebrochen. Das pietistische, verzagte alte Stuttgart hat beides nicht hervorgebracht, es blieb bei den Hafen- und Pferdemärkten, dem Christkindlesmarkt und der Maimesse in der Dorotheenstraße mit lokalem Charakter. Lediglich das 1818 von König Wilhelm I. obrigkeitlich dekretierte und damals traditionslose allherbstliche Cannstatter Volksfest mit seiner angeschlossenen landwirtschaftlichen Ausstellung ist ein letztes Aufscheinen dieser Verbindung, übrigens nur kurz nach dem ab 1812 abgehaltenen »Zentralen Landwirtschaftsfest« auf der Münchner Theresienwiese, dem Oktoberfest.

Landesausstellungen in der Gewerbehalle

Mit der Industrialisierung und der sprunghaften Entwicklung von Verkehrswesen und Kommunikation verschoben sich die politischen und wirtschaftlichen Gewichte zwischen Regentschaft und Bürgertum. Anders als etwa in Bayern erfuhr der technische und wirtschaftliche Fortschritt nicht die beherzte Unterstützung durch die Monarchie. 1881 war das Jahr, als sich das seit 1862 der Zunftordnungen ledige Handwerk nach dem Erlass des Reichsgesetzes in Fachinnungen zu organisieren begann, die Zeit der Pferdestraßenbahnen und der ersten Glühbirnen, der beschleunigten Industrialisierung Württembergs. In diesem Jahr wurde auch die Gewerbehalle eröffnet, die der städtische Baurat Wolff im Geviert Holzgarten, Kriegsbergstraße, Kanzleistraße (heute Willi-Bleicher-Straße) und Alleenstraße (heute Max-Kade-Weg) am damaligen Alleenplatz (heute Stadtgarten) errichtete. Es war also die Stadt, nicht der König, die den ersten ständigen Messeplatz Stuttgarts bauen ließ.

Middle Ages, whereas, in the city, festivals grew to become amusement fairs with a beer tent and rides but no market or trade fair. Since then, the connection between amusement fair and trade fair have been severed. Pious, slow-moving old Stuttgart produced neither, sticking to harbour and horse markets, the Christmas market and the local May market in Dorotheenstrasse. Only the Canstatt amusement fair in autumn which was decreed in 1818 by King Wilhelm I and was accompanied by an agricultural exhibition is a last sign of this connection. By the way, this was only shortly after the Oktoberfest on the Theresienwiese in Munich which has been held since 1812.

State exhibitions in the »Gewerbehalle« (hall of commerce)

With the onset of industrialisation and the sudden burgeoning of traffic and inter-regional communication, the political and economic relationship between the regency and civilian life was shifted. Unlike in Bavaria, technical and economic progress was not enthusiastically supported by the monarchy. 1881 was the year when the trades, which had been burdened with ordinances of association since 1862, began to organise themselves into specialist guilds after the imperial law was passed. It was also the time of horse-pulled trams, the first light bulbs, and the accelerated industrialisation of Württemberg. In this year, the hall of commerce (Gewerbehalle) was opened which Wolff, the municipal councillor for building at the time, erected in the square formed by Holzgarten, Kriegsbergstrasse, Kanzleistraße (today Willi-Bleicher-Strasse) and Alleenstrasse (today Max-Kade-Weg) in the former Alleenplatz (now the municipal park). It was therefore the city and not the king which built the first permanent trade fair centre in Stuttgart.

In der Gewerbehalle wurde 1881 die Reihe der Landesgewerbeausstellungen begründet, in denen das örtliche Handwerk und die noch junge Industrie Württembergs ihre Erzeugnisse präsentieren konnten. Ab 1882 war sie auch Standort der Dauerausstellung des Exportmusterlagers und Schauplatz unterschiedlicher Ausstellungen und Messen. Die Spanne reichte von der »Ausstellung für Elektrotechnik und Kunstgewerbe« 1896 über »Das Schwäbische Land« 1925 bis zur »Süddeutschen Textilbekleidungsmesse Stuttgart« 1928 und zur »Ausstellung für Ernährung und Körperpflege« 1929, von der Hunde- und der Aquarienschau bis zur Nahrungsmittelausstellung.

Beim Bau des stattlichen Gebäudes 1880 trauten sich die Stuttgarter noch nicht, richtig modern zu sein, und so wurde die 100 Meter lange Ausstellungshalle aus Eisen und Glas mit einer historistischen Umbauung in zeitgemäßem Rundbogenklassizismus verpackt. Als repräsentatives Eingangsbauwerk fungierte ein dreiachsiger Mittelpavillon mit barockem Kuppelzeltdach.

Der Platz südlich vor dem Gebäude diente als Ausstellungsfreigelände. Zur Stuttgarter Bauausstellung 1908 wurde hier neben einer »Eisenbetonhalle von Wayß & Freitag A.-G.« und dem »Haus der Stuttgarter Möbelfabrikanten« sogar eine Siedlung von Musterhäusern errichtet, einschließlich Schulpavillon und Hüttchen für die »biologische Kläranlage«. Noch vor dem Ersten Weltkrieg wurde das Freigelände durch eingeschossige Schauhallen in einem klassizierenden, vormodernen Stil umbaut.

Das Ausstellungs- und Messegelände fiel 1943 einem Bombenangriff zum Opfer und wurde nach dem Krieg anderen Zwecken zugeführt. Seit 1961 steht am Ort der Gewerbehalle die Universitätsbibliothek.

In 1881, a series of state commercial exhibitions was established in the hall of commerce, enabling local craftsmen and the still young industry of Württemberg to present their products. As of 1882, it was also the location of the permanent exhibition of the Exportmusterlager (samples of regional products) and was the scene of diverse exhibitions and trade fairs as well. The spectrum ranged from the »Ausstellung für Elektrotechnik und Kunstgewerbe« (electrical engineering and craftwork exhibition) in 1896 and the »Das Schwäbische Land« (the Swabian state) in 1925 to the »Süddeutschen Textilbekleidungsmesse Stuttgart« (south German textile clothing fair Stuttgart) in 1928, the »Ausstellung für Ernährung und Körperpflege« (exhibition for food and bodycare) in 1929 as well as dog shows, aquarium shows and food exhibitions.

When the stately building was erected in 1880, the people of Stuttgart were somewhat reluctant to undergo the transition to the really modern. The 100 metre long exhibition hall made of iron and glass was therefore packaged in a historical building development in the classical style of semicircular arches. A central pavilion with three axes and a baroque domical roof served as a prestige entrance building for the venue.

The square on the south side of the building was used as an open exhibition area. For the Stuttgart building exhibition in 1908, an estate of showcase houses, including school pavilion and little hut for the »biological sewage system«, was even erected next to a reinforced concrete hall designed by Wayss & Freitag A.-G. and the »Haus der Stuttgarter Möbelfabrikanten« (house of Stuttgart furniture manufacturers). Before the First World War, the open area was built over with single-storey exhibition halls in a classic-based, pre-modern style.

In 1943, the exhibition and trade fair site was the victim of a bombing raid and, after the war, was used for various other purposes. Since 1961, the university library has been where the old hall of commerce used to stand.

01 Gewerbehalle am Alleenplatz

Hall of commerce in Alleenplatz

02–04 Ausstellungsgelände an der Gewerbehalle mit neuen Hallen vor 1914

Exhibition area of the hall of commerce with new halls before 1914

05 Stuttgarter Bauausstellung 1908 rings um die Gewerbehalle

Stuttgart Bauausstellung 1908 (building expo) around the hall of commerce

01

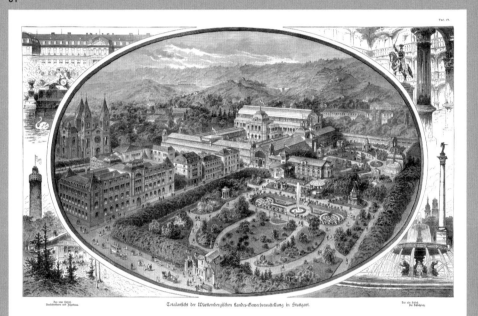

02
03

04

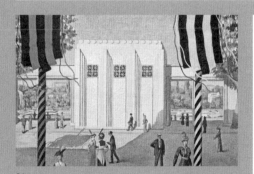

05

01 Ausstellungsgelände Killesberg,
Reichsgartenschau 1939, Wasserspiele und
hölzerne Schauhallen

Exhibition grounds in Killesberg,
Reichsgartenschau 1939 (state garden show),
fountains and wooden show halls

02 Reichsgartenschau 1939, Haupthalle
»Reichsnährstandshalle« mit monumentalem
eisernem Reichsadler

Reichsgartenschau 1939 (state garden show),
main hall called the »Reichsnährstandshalle« with
monumental imperial eagle made of iron

03 Ausstellungsgelände Killesberg 1939,
Eingangshalle

Exhibition grounds in Killesberg 1939,
entrance hall

01

02

03

Sprung auf den Killesberg

Nach dem Krieg wurde für das Stuttgarter Ausstellungswesen ein neues Kapitel aufgeschlagen. Die rasch steigenden Bodenpreise und der erwartete Flächenbedarf eines Ausstellungsgeländes legten die Verlagerung an einen peripheren Standort nahe. Der Killesberg geriet ins Blickfeld, hatte er doch bereits vor dem Krieg als Ausstellungsgelände gedient, vor allem für die Reichsgartenschau 1939, die mitten in den Kriegsvorbereitungen des Reichs als Friedensdemonstration aufgezogen wurde. Doch die martialisch-militärische Organisation bis hin zu den Baulichkeiten im neoklassizistischen Repräsentationsstil des Dritten Reichs sprach eine andere Sprache. Ein »Ehrenhof« und eine Haupthalle in pseudosakraler Erhabenheit sowie eine großzügige Ausstattung mit stählernen Reichsadlern gehörten zum signifikanten Erscheinungsbild der Schau.

1945 waren statt der Erhabenheit nur noch Trümmer und 150 Bombentrichter vorzufinden. So gab die Planung der »Deutschen Gartenschau 1950« auf dem Killesberg den Anstoß, mit dem »Höhenpark Killesberg« einen neuen Anfang zu wagen und einen ständigen Messestandort zu entwickeln. 1951 erfolgte die Gründung der »Stuttgarter Ausstellungs GmbH« als Messeveranstalter im Höhenpark Killesberg, die zunächst die Gartenschauhallen betrieb.

Schon 1952 konnten vier neue Hallen mit 10.000 Quadratmetern eröffnet werden, die entlang der Stresemannstraße entstanden waren (ursprünglich Halle 1 bis 4, in der später geänderten Nummernfolge 6.0 bis 9.0). Architekt Hellmut Weber hatte großzügig verglaste Gehäuse wunderbar einfach und überzeugend detailliert mit leichter Hand entworfen. Nur die mit Sheds gedeckte Halle 4 erhielt an der Stresemannstraße eine geschlossene Buntsandsteinfassade, die mit einem figürlichen Relief geschmückt wurde. Die Qualitäten dieser ersten Nachkriegsbauten können auch heute noch überzeugen und lassen sie, im Unterschied zu den späteren Erweiterungen, als Kulturdenkmale erhaltenswert erscheinen.

The move to Killesberg

After the war, a new chapter in Stuttgart's exhibition history commenced. Due to the rapidly rising prices for land and the expected space needed for an exhibition site, a move to a location on the periphery of the city seemed a reasonable idea. The Killesberg area came under consideration, having already served as an exhibition site before the war, in particular for the 1939 imperial garden show which had been organised as a demonstration of the will to peace right in the middle of war preparations. However, the martial and militaristic organisation which permeated all aspects of the show, including structures built in the bombastic neoclassical style of the Third Reich, spoke a completely different language. An »Ehrenhof« (courtyard of honour) and a main hall of pseudo-religious grandeur as well as generous quantities of the Reich's typical eagle statues belonged to the characterising image of the show.

In 1945, nothing was left of the grandeur, except for rubble and 150 bomb craters. The plans to hold the »Deutschen Gartenschau 1950« (German garden show 1950) in Killesberg were therefore a reason to attempt a new beginning with the »Höhenpark Killesberg« (Killesberg park) and develop a permanent trade fair location there. In 1951, a company calling itself »Stuttgarter Ausstellungs GmbH« was established as the trade fair organiser in Killesberg park and initially provided halls for garden shows.

Only one year later in 1952, four new halls with a floor area of 10,000 square metres were opened along Stresemannstrasse (originally halls 1 to 4, whose numbers were changed later to halls 6.0 to 9.0). Architect Hellmut Weber had used a light hand to design large glazed structures with wonderfully simple but convincing details. Along Stresemannstrasse, only hall 4, with its sawtooth roof, had a closed mottled-sandstone facade, decorated with a figurative relief. The qualities of these first new buildings after the war are still impressive today and, in contrast to the later extensions, are worthy of preservation as historic buildings.

Deutlich mehr Möglichkeiten hatte Weber dann 1955 bei der größeren »Sägedachhalle«. Der luftige Eingangspavillon, charakteristische Sheds und die gestaffelte Ostfassade sowie im Inneren eine Galerie mit dem dynamischen Schwung der fünfziger Jahre prägten lange Zeit das Bild der Messe. Zwei niedrige Anbauten dieser Halle 4.0 an der Westseite, ursprünglich Westhalle Süd- und Nordflügel, erhielten später die Nummern 1.0 und 3.0. Eine ebenfalls elegant geschwungene Verbindungshalle unter dem Vorplatz nutzte die Höhendifferenz und verband die neue mit den bisherigen Hallen.

Weniger harmonisch gerieten 1961 Webers Verwaltungsgebäude der Messegesellschaft und das Kongresszentrum A, die westlich an die Sägedachhalle und im Hofbereich angestückelt wurden.

Einen großen Schritt voran machte man mit der Erweiterung im Jahr 1965. Mit der Halle 10.0 gelang der Brückenschlag über die Stresemannstraße zum Anschluss dreier weiterer Hallen 11.0 bis 14.0 (die 13 wurde aus Rücksicht vor abergläubischen Ausstellern übergangen), die architektonisch anspruchslos und, dem Bedarf der Aussteller angepasst, nurmehr spärlich befenstert ausfielen. Durch die Erweiterungsbauten jenseits der Straße konnte der Park selbst geschont werden. Gleichzeitig veränderte man das Erscheinungsbild der Eingangsfront an der Straße Am Kochenhof entscheidend. Doch die Reihe knallroter Kassenhäuschen, durch ein dunkelrotes Sheddach aus Welleternit überdeckelt, war wohl zu zeitgeistig, um länger Bestand zu haben.

In 1955, Weber had considerably more latitude in the case of the larger hall with its sawtooth roof. The airy entrance pavilion, the characteristic sawtooth roof and the staggered east facade as well as the interior gallery with the dynamic curve typical of the 1950s were characterising features of the trade fair for a long time after. Two low extensions to hall 4.0 on the west side, originally the south and north wings of the west hall, were later given the numbers 1.0 and 3.0. A connecting hall, which also featured an elegant curve and was located beneath the forecourt, used the height difference and joined up the new hall to the old ones that already existed.

In 1961, Weber's administration building and congress centre A were less harmonious. They were added on piecemeal to the west side of the hall and in the courtyard area.

A large step forward was taken with the extension carried out in 1965. The erection of hall 10.0 enables Stresemannstrasse to be crossed to connect three additional halls, numbers 11.0 to 14.0 (the number 13 was avoided so as not to upset superstitious exhibitors). The latter were architecturally unassuming and, in accordance with the needs of the exhibitors, had a very small window area. By erecting the extension buildings on the other side of the street, the park itself was left untouched. At the same time, the appearance of the entrance area was changed decisively in the street Am Kochenhof. But it appeared that the row of bright red little ticket houses covered by a shed roof made of corrugated asbestos cement was too close a reflection of the spirit of the time to last very long.

01 Messegelände Killesberg, Ausstellungshallen 1 und 2 (später 6.0 und 7.0) um 1952

Exhibition grounds in Killesberg, exhibition halls 1 and 2 (later 6.0 and 7.0), around 1952

02 Eingang Halle 4 (»Sägedachhalle«) Am Kochenhof

Entrance to hall 4 (»Sägedachhalle« = hall with sawtooth roof) Am Kochenhof

03 Ausstellungshalle 2

Exhibition hall 2

04 Messegelände Killesberg 1955 mit Halle 4 (»Sägedachhalle«)

Trade fair grounds in Killesberg 1955 with hall 4 (»Sägedachhalle« = hall with sawtooth roof)

05 Hallen 2 und 3 (später 7.0 und 9.0) entlang der Stresemannstraße

Halls 2 and 3 (later 7.0 and 9.0) along Stresemannstrasse

01

02
03

04

05

01 Messegelände Killesberg
von Süden, 2003

Trade fair venue in Killesberg
from the south, 2003

02 Rote Kassenhäuschen Am Kochenhof
(genannt »Hüttenwerk«)

Red ticket kiosks Am Kochenhof

03 Eingangsrotunde und Halle 5.2 von 1988

Entrance rotunda and hall 5.2 from 1988

04 Hallen 6.0 und 7.0 entlang der
Stresemannstraße

Halls 6.0 and 7.0 in Stresemannstrasse

05 Halle 5.2, 1982

Hall 5.2, 1982

01

02
03

04

05

Die Messe stößt an ihre Grenzen

Bald hatten sie wieder ausgedient, denn bei den letzten Erweiterungsschüben 1982 und 1988 durch die Architekten Bidlingmaier, Egenhofer und Dübbers wurde ein kreisrunder gläserner Pavillon auf den Vorplatz gestellt, der die Kassenhäuschen aufnahm und als Informations- und Pressezentrum fungierte. Im Zug der letzten Erweiterungen wurde der Raum zwischen den Ursprungshallen endgültig zugebaut. Die Sägedachhalle, das architektonisch wertvollste Bauwerk der Messe, verschwand vollends hinter der vorgebauten Halle 5.2. Die Wasserspiele wurden durch die Halle 5.0 ersetzt und der übrige Platz durch das Congress Centrum B und Erweiterungen der Hallen 6.0 und 7.0 bis auf einen Anlieferhof aufgefüllt. Durch schrittweise Erweiterungen mit zunehmend mediocer wirkenden Zubauten wurde dem Höhenpark im Lauf der Jahre Stück für Stück wertvolle Fläche entzogen. Immerhin sorgte die Messe für einen nach wie vor repräsentativen, breiten Eingang zum Park über die unterirdische Halle 5.0 hinweg und begleitet von der leichten, gewächshausartigen Architektur der Vorbauten der Halle 5.2 einerseits und des Congress Centrums mit seinem Parkrestaurant andererseits.

Naturgemäß wurden die funktionalen Verhältnisse und die Verkehrserschließung der beengten und labyrinthischen Örtlichkeiten immer prekärer. 1989 hatte das Messegelände mit 54.500 Quadratmeter Hallenfläche seinen letzten Ausbaustand erreicht und war damit buchstäblich an seine Grenzen gestoßen. Weder waren räumliche Erweiterungsmöglichkeiten gegeben, noch gab es für Infrastruktur und Verkehrserschließung weiteren Spielraum. Zudem waren die Belastung und die Unduldsamkeit der Nachbarschaft in den umgebenden Wohngebieten auf ein nicht länger vertretbares Maß gewachsen. Die Verkehrssituation beeinträchtigte auch die Funktion der Messe, denn die Aussteller klagten über Parkplatzmangel, Verkehrschaos und sieben Kilometer lange Staus bis hinauf zu Kräherwald und Schattenring.

How the trade fair site came up against its limits

Soon, they were out of favour. When the last extensions were added in 1982 and 1988 by architects Bidlingmaier, Egenhofer and Dübbers, a circular glass pavilion was placed on the forecourt. It accommodated the little ticket houses and served as an information and press centre at the same time. In the course of the final extensions, the space between the original halls was finally built over. The hall with the saw-tooth roof, the architecturally most valuable building of the trade fair location, disappeared completely behind hall 5.2. The water fountains were replaced with hall 5.0 and the remaining space was filled with congress centre B and extensions of halls 6.0 and 7.0 plus a delivery yard. As a result of gradual extensions with increasingly mediocre buildings being added on, valuable areas of Killesberg park were gradually encroached on over the years. Nevertheless, the trade fair venue still provided a prestigious, wide entrance to the park beyond the underground hall number 5.0, accompanied by the light, greenhouse-like architecture of the front buildings of hall 5.2 and the congress centre with its park restaurant.

The functional interrelationships and access to transport connections and roads naturally became more and more precarious given the constricted and labyrinthine layout of the site. In 1989, the trade fair site had reached its maximum size of 54,500 square metres of hall space and had therefore literally come up against its limits in terms of space. There was neither room for further extensions nor was there any more latitude for infrastructure and transport connections. Moreover, the stress on the neighbouring areas and the refusal of the surrounding residents to put up with the situation any longer had reached unmanageable proportions. The traffic situation was also impairing the workings of the trade fair location as the exhibitors complained about the lack of parking space, the traffic chaos and seven kilometre-long traffic jams as far as Kräherwald and Schattenring.

Umsatzbezogen stand die Messe Stuttgart um die Jahrtausendwende noch auf dem siebten Rang (einschließlich Hanns-Martin-Schleyer-Halle und Kultur- & Kongresszentrum Liederhalle) und war im Jahr 2003 bereits auf Platz neun abgerutscht. 2005 besetzte man in der Rangliste der Hallenkapazitäten Rang 14, knapp hinter Augsburg, ein Zustand, den in der prosperierenden Wirtschaftsregion Mittlerer Neckar niemand für akzeptabel hielt.

Eine Erfolgsgeschichte war das Messegelände auf dem Killesberg aufgrund von Zuschnitt und Lage nur eingeschränkt gewesen. Und so wurden die Proteste der Anwohner und Rufe der Messegesellschaft nach einem neuen Standort lauter und führten schließlich zum Befreiungsschlag. Land und Stadt beschlossen gemeinsam, eine neue Messe zu bauen, die »Landesmesse Baden-Württemberg«, wie das Projekt »Neue Messe Stuttgart« anfangs firmierte. Nach 125 Jahren Messebetrieb in städtischer Obhut, zuletzt durch die stadteigene Stuttgarter Messe- und Kongress GmbH (SMK), wird der 50-prozentige Einstieg des Landes durch den seit 1. Januar 2007 gültigen Unternehmensnamen Landesmesse Stuttgart GmbH (LMS) dokumentiert.

In terms of sales, the Stuttgart trade fair centre in Killesberg was still in seventh place at the turn of the millennium (including Hanns-Martin-Schleyer-Halle and the Liederhalle culture and congress centre) but, by 2003, had already slipped down to position 9 in the rankings. In 2005, it occupied position 14 in the ranking of hall capacities, just behind Augsburg – a state of affairs that was no longer acceptable in the prosperous middle-Neckar industrial region.

The Killesberg trade fair site was only a limited success due to its layout and position. The protests of local residents and the calls of the trade fair company for a completely new location therefore became louder and louder until they finally led to an act of liberation. The state and the city decided to build a new trade fair centre together, namely the »Landesmesse Baden-Württemberg« (The Baden-Württemberg State Trade Fair Centre), as the »Neue Messe Stuttgart« (New Stuttgart Trade Fair Centre) was originally called. After 125 years under the auspices of the city and, at the end, of the city's own company Stuttgarter Messe- und Kongress GmbH (SMK), the 50 per cent participation of the state is now reflected in the name of the company responsible for the centre, namely Landesmesse Stuttgart GmbH (LMS), which has been applicable since 1 January 2007.

01 Messegelände Killesberg,
Eingangsrotunde Am Kochenhof 1988

Trade fair grounds in Killesberg,
entrance rotunda Am Kochenhof 1988

02 Halle 8, später 8.0

Hall 8, later 8.0

03 Brückenhalle 10.0 über
die Stresemannstraße 1965

Bridge hall 10.0 over
Stresemannstrasse 1965

04 Hallen 11.0, 12.0 und 14.0 an der
Oskar-Schlemmer-Straße
(»Allianzhallen«), erbaut 1965

Halls 11.0, 12.0 and 14.0
in Oskar-Schlemmer-Strasse
(»Allianz halls«), built in 1965

01

02

03

04

Tanzende Hallen, Kreis oder Kamm
Der Architektenwettbewerb und seine Ergebnisse

Dancing halls, circle or mountain ridge
The architectural competition and its results

Tanzende Hallen, Kreis oder Kamm
Der Architektenwettbewerb und seine Ergebnisse

Dancing halls, circle or mountain ridge
The architectural competition and its results

Zweimal hat man den Blick übers Land schweifen lassen, um nach geeigneten Standorten für die neue Landesmesse Ausschau zu halten. 94 potenzielle Standorte wurden unter die Lupe genommen. Einer erwies sich als unübertrefflich, der Krautacker zwischen »Echterdinger Ei«, Autobahn A 8 und Flughafen Stuttgart. Dass sich die politische Entscheidung für diesen Ort bis hin zum Gesetzgebungsverfahren für das Messegesetz nicht als Kinderspiel erweisen sollte, hat niemanden überrascht. Dagegen fiel die Auswahl und Entscheidung für einen architektonischen Entwurf eher leicht, wenngleich lange Zeit nicht alle Beteiligten am selben Strang ziehen wollten. Ein Wettbewerbsverfahren dieser Größenordnung stellt jedenfalls ein Marathonunterfangen dar.

Als sich die damit befassten Gremien bei Land und Messegesellschaft über eine Programmformulierung geeinigt hatten, lobte die Projektgesellschaft Neue Messe für den Zulassungsbereich EWR (Europäischer Wirtschaftsraum) einen einstufigen, interdisziplinären, offenen Realisierungswettbewerb in zwei Bearbeitungsphasen aus, um zu einem konkreten Architekturentwurf zu kommen. Das Verfahren wurde anonym durchgeführt (Regelverfahren nach GRW 95). Die Architektenteams sollten sich jeweils mit einem Garten- und Landschaftsarchitekten zu einer Arbeitsgemeinschaft zusammenschließen, was sich für das Verfahren durchaus als bedeutsam erweisen sollte. Für die zweite Phase wurde die Hinzuziehung von Fachberatern für Tragwerk, technische Ausrüstung und Verkehrsanlagen empfohlen.

Als Vorprüfer und Betreuer des mit einer Preissumme von 1,2 Millionen DM ausgestatteten Wettbewerbs fungierten in der ersten Phase die I'RW AG München und das Büro für Stadt- und Regionalplanung, Projektbetreuung und Architektur aus Stuttgart. Nach der zweiten Phase kam Drees & Sommer hinzu.

108 Arbeiten waren durch das prominent besetzte Preisgericht unter dem Vorsitz von Fred Angerer zu beurteilen. Weiterhin saßen im Preisgericht als Fachpreisrichter die Architekten und Planer Albert Ackermann, Jürgen A. Adam, Fritz Auer, Ulrich Bauer, Reinald Ensslin, Francine Houben, Hans W. Liebert, Wilfried Moog, Wolfgang Riehle, Matthias Sauerbruch, Brigitte Schmelzer und

In two separate sweeps, the region was scanned carefully in search of suitable locations for the new state trade fair centre. A total of 94 potential locations were placed under the microscope, one of which stood clearly out from all the rest: the agricultural land between the »Echterdinger Ei« (egg-shaped piece of land in Echterdingen), the A8 motorway and Stuttgart's airport. No-one was surprised by the fact that the political decision-making process in favour of this location was anything but simple in the time leading up to the legislative procedure for the associated trade fair law. In contrast, the choice of an architectural design was relatively easy, even though, for a long time, not everyone was willing to pull together. A competition of this size is in any case a marathon undertaking.

When the committees for the state and the trade fair company had come to an agreement on formulation of a programme, Projektgesellschaft Neue Messe sent out an invitation to participate in a single-stage, interdisciplinary and open competition for the certification area of the EEC (European Economic Union). The competition was to take place in two phases in order to finally arrive at a concrete architectural design. The procedure was conducted anonymously (standard procedure according to the principles and guidelines for competitions GRW 95). The teams of architects were to join forces with landscape architects to form work groups. This turned out to be very significant for the procedure as a whole. For the second phase, it was recommended that specialist consultants be brought in for the load-bearing structure, the technical equipment and the traffic systems required.

In the first phase, I'RW AG Munich and the Büro für Stadt- und Regionalplanung, Projektbetreuung und Architektur (office for urban and regional planning, project support and architecture) from Stuttgart acted as preliminary judges and contact offices for the competition, which carried total prize money of DM 1.2 million. After the second phase, they were joined by Drees & Sommer.

Seite 032
Neue Messe Stuttgart, Wettbewerbsmodell
Wulf & Partner 1999

Page 032
New Stuttgart Trade Fair Centre,
competition model of Wulf & Partner 1999

Peter Zlonicky, sowie als Fachpreisrichter DB-Geschäftsführer Reimar Baur, Bürgermeister Dr. Dieter Blessing, FSG-Geschäftsführer Georg Fundel, SMK-Geschäftsführer Dr. Walter Gehring, Bürgermeister Matthias Hahn, Staatssekretär Dr. Horst Mehrländer, Umwelt- und Verkehrsminister Ulrich Müller, Verbandsvorsitzender Eberhardt Palmer, Oberbürgermeister Dr. Wolfgang Schuster und Ministerpräsident Erwin Teufel.

Vorgegebene Idee

Die Teilnehmer am Wettbewerb sahen sich mit einer 126 Seiten starken Auslobung konfrontiert sowie mit einem städtebaulichen Konzept, das als ungewohnt weit entwickelter und bis hin zu Schwebebahn und Personenbeförderungsbändern ausgearbeiteter Testentwurf vorgestellt wurde. Das Stuttgarter Büro a.d.s. Architektur – Design – Selzer pflanzte damit aber auch Ideen in die Köpfe der Teilnehmer, von denen sich die meisten nicht lösen konnten. So positionierten sie eine Plaza mit Haupteingang an die Stelle des vorgesehenen ICE-Bahnhofs gegenüber der Flughafenterminals 1 und 2 und legten von dort aus die Hauptachse der Messe Richtung Nordwesten parallel zur Autobahn. Zehn die Autobahn überbrückende Parkhäuser ergaben eine Reihe, die fast so lang war wie die Messe selbst.

57 Teilnehmer, also mehr als die Hälfte, hatten sich in der ersten Phase dieses städtebaulichen Grundschemas bedient, während 28 die Hauptachse parallel zum Flughafen legten. Einige Hybridformen mit gebogener Hauptachse, mit zwei oder drei Achsen, das Marktplatzprinzip oder ein Cluster tanzender Hallen erweiterten das Spektrum der Vorschläge. Kreisförmig angeordnete oder unregelmäßig verteilte Hallen blieben Einzelfälle und nur das Frankfurter Team Schneider + Schumacher bot eine flächendeckende, von Pilzstützen getragene Dachstruktur als Lösung.

A total of 108 submissions had to be assessed by the prize jury, which had many prominent members and Fred Angerer as the foreman. Other members of the jury included architects and planners Albert Ackermann, Jürgen A. Adam, Fritz Auer, Ulrich Bauer, Reinald Ensslin, Francine Houben, Hans W. Liebert, Wilfried Moog, Wolfgang Riehle, Matthias Sauerbruch, Brigitte Schmelzer and Peter Zlonicky, as well as specialist members Reimar Baur (CEO of German Rail), Mayor Dr. Dieter Blessing, Georg Fundel (head of FSG), Dr. Walter Gehring (head of SMK), Mayor Matthias Hahn, State Secretary Dr. Horst Mehrländer, Minister of the Environment and Transport Ulrich Müller, Association Chairman Eberhardt Palmer, Lord Mayor Dr. Wolfgang Schuster and Minister President Erwin Teufel.

A pre-determined idea

The participants in the competition were confronted with a 126-page description of what was expected of them as well as with an urban planning concept. The latter was presented as a draft test design. It had been elaborated to an unusual degree of detail and included a suspension railway and moving walkways. The Stuttgart architect's office, a.d.s. Architektur – Design – Selzer, which had drawn up the concept, thus planted ideas in the heads of the participants from which most of them were unable to free themselves. For example, they positioned a plaza with main entrance in place of the envisaged ICE railway station opposite airport terminals 1 and 2 and, from there, placed the main axis of the trade fair centre in a north-west direction parallel to the motorway. Ten multi-storey car parks bridging the motorway resulted in a row of structures that was almost as long as the trade fair centre itself.

In the first phase, 57 participants, in other words more than half, had made use of this underlying urban planning scheme, whereas 28 placed the main axis parallel to the airport. Some hybrid forms with a curved main axis, with two or three axes, a market square approach or a cluster of »dancing« halls expanded the range of proposals that were made at the time. Halls arranged in a circle or irregularly distributed remained isolated cases and only the Frankfurt team Schneider + Schumacher offered an overall roof structure supported by mushroom-shaped columns as a solution.

Der zweite Durchgang

Dieser Entwurf war der außergewöhnlichste unter den 30 auserwählten, die in die zweite Phase einer Überarbeitung geschickt wurden (und schied dort im zweiten Rundgang aus). 20 Arbeiten zeigten eine doppelte Kammstruktur, wobei nur bei dem später siegreichen Entwurf die Hauptachse parallel zum Flughafen gelegt wurde. Zwei Teams staffelten die Hallen entlang einer Mittelachse und sieben Bearbeiter ordneten die Hallen um einen zentralen Platz an oder wählten eine kompaktere Disposition. Wie sich in der weiteren Beratung zeigte, spielt die nicht unerhebliche Neigung des Geländes eine große Rolle. Fünf Teams ignorierten sie und planierten den Hallenbereich, wie es das Programm vorgeschlagen hatte. Bei 22 Arbeiten liegen die Hallen auf zwei verschiedenen Ebenen und bei zwei Entwürfen, darunter der siegreiche, ist das Gelände mehrfach terrassiert, wie es im Programm eigentlich nicht vorgesehen war. Die Hälfte der Bearbeiter nahm die Anregung auf, Parkhäuser über der Autobahn anzuordnen.

Drei erste Preise (je 240.000 DM), drei zweite Preise (je 100.000 DM) und drei Ankäufe (je 60.000 DM) wählte die Jury schließlich aus den 29 abgegebenen Arbeiten. Die angekauften Entwürfe von KSP Engel und Zimmermann aus Frankfurt am Main mit einer quadratisch-kompakten Anlage und des Londoners Richard Horden mit zwei gestaffelt verschobenen Hallenreihen tanzten gewissermaßen aus der Reihe. Doch bereits der dritte Ankauf von Hascher + Jehle aus Berlin zeigte die unter den ausgezeichneten Arbeiten überwiegende Doppelkammstruktur entlang der Autobahn, die auch von den zweiten Preisträgern ARP Stuttgart, von Gerkan Marg und Partner aus Hamburg und den Siegern in der ersten Preisgruppe Theo Hotz aus Zürich mit Raderschall Landschaftsarchitekten, Meilen, und Kaup, Scholz, Jesse + Partner aus München mit Landschaftsarchitekt Peter Kluska, München, gewählt wurde. Obermeyer Planen + Beraten, Stuttgart/München (ein zweiter Preis), bildeten mit zwei Reihen Messehallen und der Hochhalle ein Dreieck, in dessen Mitte ein »Messpark« Verbindung zum Filderfreiraum nach Nordwesten haben sollte.

The second round

This design was the most unusual among the 30 which were selected and sent into the second round where their designs were to be refined (it was knocked out in this second stage). 20 submissions featured a double structure in the form of a mountain ridge, whereby only the design which later won the competition placed the main axis parallel to the airport. Two teams staggered the halls along a central axis while seven positioned the halls around a central square or selected a more compact arrangement. As became apparent during further discussions, the not inconsiderable slope of the terrain played an important role. Five teams ignored it and planned the hall area as had been suggested by the predetermined concept. In 22 of the submissions, the halls were on two different levels and, in two designs, including the winning one, the site is terraced in contrast to the initial proposal. Half of the contestants took up the idea of placing the multi-storey car parks over the motorway.

Three first prize winners (each winning DM 240,000), three second prize winners (DM 100,000 each) and three bought-in designs (DM 60,000 each) were finally selected from the 29 submissions. The bought-in designs from KSP Engel und Zimmermann, Frankfurt am Main, involving a square-shaped compact layout and that of Richard Horden from London featuring two staggered rows of halls stood somewhat apart from the rest. However, the third bought-in design from Hascher + Jehle, Berlin, incorporated the double mountain-ridge structure along the motorway like most of the other submissions that won prizes. This approach was also selected by the winners of the second prize, ARP Stuttgart, Gerkan Marg und Partner from Hamburg, and the winners in the first prize group, Theo Hotz from Zurich with Raderschall Landschaftsarchitekten, Meilen, and Kaup, Scholz, Jesse + Partner from Munich with landscape architect Kluska from Munich. Obermeyer Planen + Beraten, Stuttgart/Munich (winner of a second prize) aligned two rows of trade fair halls and the high hall to form a triangle, in the middle of which a »trade fair park« linked to the free Filder area to the north west was to be located.

01 Neue Messe Stuttgart, Wettbewerbsmodell
Wulf & Partner, ein 1. Preis

New Stuttgart Trade Fair Centre,
competition model of Wulf & Partner, a 1st prize

02 Kaup, Scholz, Jesse + Partner, München,
mit Landschaftsarchitekt
Peter Kluska, München, ein 1. Preis

Kaup, Scholz, Jesse + Partner, Munich,
with landscape architect
Peter Kluska, Munich, a 1st prize

03 Theo Hotz, Zürich, mit Raderschall
Landschaftsarchitekten, Meilen, ein 1. Preis

Theo Hotz, Zürich, with Raderschall
Landschaftsarchitekten, Meilen, a 1st prize

04 Obermeyer Planen + Beraten, Stuttgart/München,
mit Lehnhoff + Partner, Landschaftsarchitekten
und Stadtplaner Beratende Ingenieure, Stuttgart,
ein 2. Preis

Obermeyer Planen + Beraten, Stuttgart/Munich,
with Lehnhoff + Partner, landscape architects,
urban planners and consulting engineers, Stuttgart,
a 2nd prize

05 Von Gerkan Marg und Partner, Hamburg, mit
Bertel K. Bruun, Hamburg/Kopenhagen, ein 2. Preis

Von Gerkan Marg and Partner, Hamburg, with
Bertel K. Bruun, Hamburg/Copenhagen, a 2nd prize

01

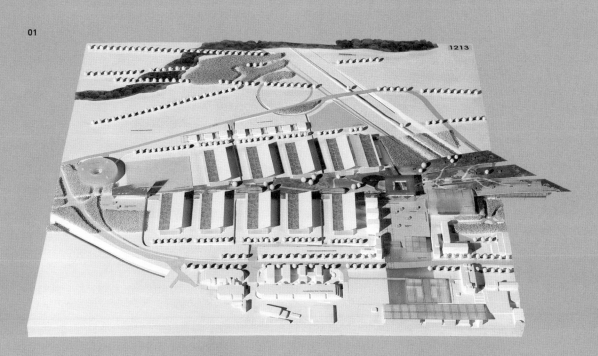

02

03

04

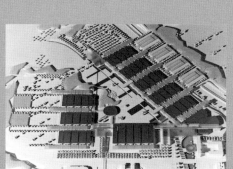

05

Die größten Veränderungen in der abschließenden Überarbeitungsphase der drei ersten Preise erfuhr der Entwurf von Wulf & Partner mit Adler + Olesch, Landschaftsplaner aus Nürnberg. Eine der Standardhallen fiel weg und eine weitere wanderte von der Südreihe in die Nordreihe. Vor allem jedoch wurde das Congresscenter von seiner isolierten Position östlich der Plaza nach Westen in die südliche Hallenreihe gerückt, mit dem Ergebnis, dass es besser an die Messeaktivitäten angeschlossen ist und seine Ausstellungshalle als Halle 2 in den normalen Messebetrieb integriert werden kann. Erleichtert wurde auch die Anbindung des Parkhauses über die Plaza an den Flughafen.

Vor dem dritten Akt die Kostenschätzung
Als Grundlage für die endgültige Entscheidung des Preisgerichts diente eine von Drees & Sommer vorgelegte Kostenschätzung der drei in die Endphase gekommenen Entwürfe, in der die Bau- und Planungskosten der Hochbauten, der Außenanlage und der internen Erschließungswege ermittelt wurden. Der Blick nach Leipzig und München zeigte im Übrigen, dass die prognostizierten Kosten für die Neue Messe Stuttgart im Bereich der dortigen vergleichbaren neuen Messeanlagen liegen.

Generell betrachtet, schnitt der Entwurf von Theo Hotz mit 1,213 Millionen DM am günstigsten ab, gefolgt von Kaup, Scholz, Jesse + Partner mit 1,247 Millionen DM (+ 3 Prozent) und Wulf & Partner mit 1,298 Millionen DM (+ 7 Prozent). Wesentliche Unterschiede machten die Kostenschätzer bei den Messehallen aus, bei denen Kaup mit 6 Prozent und Wulf mit 8 Prozent über den Kosten des mit einem konventionellen Tragwerk ausgestatteten Entwurfs Hotz lagen, sowie vor allem beim Parken, wobei Hotz um 19 Prozent und Wulf mit dem anfänglich dreifingrigen Parkhaus über die Autobahn um stattliche 58 Prozent über dem Vorschlag Kaup lagen. Günstigere Werte erreichte Wulf im Bereich Eingänge/Erschließung.

The biggest changes in the final refining phase of the three winners of a first prize were made to the design of Wulf & Partner with Adler + Olesch, landscape planners from Nuremberg. One of the standard halls was removed and another changed place from the south row to the north row. Above all, however, the congress centre was moved from its isolated position to the east of the plaza towards the west and into the south row of halls. This meant that it was more effectively linked up to the trade fair activities and that its exhibition hall, namely hall 2, could be integrated into normal trade fair operations. Access to the airport from the multi-storey car park via the plaza was also facilitated.

Cost estimate as a prelude to act three of the drama
An estimate of the costs of the three designs that had reached the final phase was presented by Drees & Sommer. It listed the construction and planning costs for the high-rise structures, the outdoor installations and the internal connecting paths. A consideration of Leipzig and Munich showed that the costs forecast for the New Stuttgart Trade Fair Centre were about the same as those for comparable new trade fair venues in those cities.

Considered within a general framework, the design of Theo Hotz was the least expensive at DM 1.213 million, followed by Kaup, Scholz, Jesse + Partner at DM 1.247 million (+ 3 per cent) and Wulf & Partner at DM 1.298 million (+ 7 per cent). The cost assessors arrived at considerably different sums for the trade fair halls, where Kaup was 6 per cent and Wulf was 8 per cent above the costs of the Hotz design, which envisaged a conventional load-bearing structure. But the main differences were in respect of the parking facilities; Hotz was 19 per cent above Kaup's proposal and Wulf, with the multi-storey car park spanning the motorway, was a huge 58 per cent above Kaup's proposal. Wulf achieved more favourable figures in respect of the entrances/accessways.

Einstimmiges Votum

Als das Preisgericht am 11. Februar 2000 seine Sitzung beschloss, konnte der Vorsitzende Professor Fred Angerer von einem einstimmigen Votum für den Entwurf Wulf & Partner / Adler + Olesch berichten. Die Befürworter der »saloppen, genialischen Lösung« (Angerer) hatten sich gegen die Protagonisten der pragmatischeren und kostenmäßig etwas günstigeren Entwürfe durchgesetzt. Der intensivere Landschaftsbezug, der geringere Flächenverbrauch, die kürzeren Wege und die bessere Zuordnung des Parkhauses zum Flughafen waren gewichtige Argumente. Im Urteil der Fachpreisrichter kam offenkundig mit großem Gewicht die naturgemäß schwieriger zu bemessende ästhetische Komponente hinzu, die Signifikanz und Einmaligkeit der Anlage, die der Messegesellschaft letztlich bei Imagepflege und Markenbildung hilfreich sein wird.

Mit der unmissverständlichen Empfehlung, den gekürten Entwurf nun auch zu realisieren, gab das Preisgericht das Verfahren an die Politiker zurück – die sich denn auch unmittelbar nach dem Preisgericht zur internen Beratung zurückzogen.

Die Presse reagierte weitgehend positiv und verhalten optimistisch auf das Ergebnis. Doch dass nun nicht gleich die Bagger würden anrücken können, ließen die ersten Reaktionen aus den Reihen der Messegegner erahnen, die das Ergebnis als »PR-Aktion« abtaten, auf die ungedeckten Kosten verwiesen und erklärten, die geplante Messe bleibe ein Luftschloss. Nun war das Feld für die Juristen bereitet, die den Grundsatzstreit um die Messe zu entscheiden und den »Filderkrimi« zu lösen hatten. Parallel dazu und unbeirrt wurden die Planungen von der Projektgesellschaft und den Architekten weitergetrieben.

Das umfangreiche und komplexe Wettbewerbsverfahren um eines der größten deutschen Bauprojekte seit der Jahrtausendwende war jedenfalls zügig und reibungslos und mit einem klaren Ergebnis, das im Anschluss realisiert wurde, durchgeführt worden – keine Selbstverständlichkeit im deutschen Wettbewerbswesen!

A unanimous vote

When the prize jury completed its session on 11 February, 2000, the foreman of the jury, Professor Fred Angerer, reported that the vote had been unanimously in favour of the design submitted by Wulf & Partner / Adler + Olesch. Those who preferred the »casual yet brilliant solution« (Angerer) had won out against the advocates of the more pragmatic and somewhat less expensive designs. The closer involvement with the surrounding landscape, the lower amount of space needed, the shorter distances involved and better alignment of the multi-storey car park in relation to the airport were convincing arguments. In the verdict of the specialist judges, the aesthetic component, which is naturally more difficult to assess, was clearly a considerable factor. The significance and uniqueness of the project will, after all, help the company in charge of the trade fair centre in its efforts aimed at branding and promoting the centre's image.

With an unmistakeable recommendation that the prize winning design should now be adopted, the prize jury passed the ball back to the politicians, who withdrew for internal consultations immediately after the verdict was made known.

The reaction of the press was mostly positive and reservedly optimistic. But the first reactions from opponents of the trade fair centre were a sign that it would be some time before the excavators could be brought in. They dismissed the result as a »PR move«, pointed out the hidden costs and declared that the trade fair centre would remain nothing but a white elephant. The way was thus prepared for the jury members who had to decide the fundamental dispute and resolve the situation once and for all. At the same time and undistracted, the plans of the architects and the company responsible for the project went ahead.

The extensive and complex procedure involved in the competition for one of the largest German construction projects since the start of the new millennium was conducted quickly and smoothly, ending with an undisputed result that was subsequently implemented in practice – quite an achievement given the usual wrangling associated with other such competitions in Germany!

setzt den Wilden nicht die Messe an die Kehle

Protest gegen
die Messe

Die Geschichte des
Widerstands
auf den Fildern

Protest against
the trade fair centre

The history
of resistance in
the Filder area

Michael Ohnewald

Protest gegen die Messe
Die Geschichte des Widerstands auf den Fildern

Protest against the trade fair centre
The history of resistance in the Filder area

Die Geschichte des Widerstands gegen die Messe lässt sich aus mindestens drei verschiedenen Blickwinkeln erzählen. Da sind zum einen die Menschen, die von ihr unmittelbar betroffen sind, solche wie Karl Kizele und Walter Stäbler. Viele Jahre haben sie den millionenschweren Ausstellungskomplex bekämpft, weil er ihre Existenz bedrohte. Bauern wie sie empfinden das, was ihnen mit der Messe widerfahren ist, als Drama. Und wie fast alle Dramen beginnt auch dieses mit der Liebe. In ihrem Fall ist es die Liebe zur Scholle.

Man könnte die Geschichte über den Widerstand aber auch mit Leinfelden-Echterdingen beginnen, jener Stadt, die manchmal an das kleine umzingelte Dorf in Gallien erinnert, das sich gegen feindliche Übermacht wehrt, gegen hauptstädtischen Unverstand und gegen Eingriffe in die kommunale Planungshoheit. Der Vergleich mit dem Dorf in Gallien bietet sich an, weil der Ehapa-Verlag, der reich wurde durch den Krieger Asterix, früher in der Stadt ein großes Büro betrieben hat. Inzwischen hat es Ehapa nach Berlin verschlagen, geblieben ist in Leinfelden-Echterdingen der Belagerungszustand. Die 36.000 Einwohner zählende Stadt hat sich vehement gegen die neue Messe gestemmt und war dabei nicht kleinlich. Mehr als 2,5 Millionen Euro wurden für Kampagnen, Gutachten und Anwälte ausgegeben. Genutzt hat es nichts.

Schließlich könnte man die Geschichte des Widerstands auch an der Filderebene festmachen, die ins Fadenkreuz der Planer geraten ist, lange bevor es um eine neue Messe fürs Land ging. Das bietet sich an, weil die Dinge komplizierter sind, als es den Anschein hat, und weil sich jene, die dort leben, bis heute schwertun mit dem gnadenlosen Strukturwandel im Ballungsraum. Viele von ihnen haben sich der Schutzgemeinschaft Filder angeschlossen, einer der ältesten Bürgerinitiativen Deutschlands, die sich gegen den Expansionsdrang der Moderne wehrt und deren ungezügelten Appetit auf immer neue Äcker. Lange vor der Messe ist dieser Appetit erwacht. 1967 wuchs er sich zum Heißhunger aus. Der Gerlach-Plan lag auf den Tischen der Regierenden. Er hatte die Vergrößerung des Echterdinger Flughafens von 272 auf 1000 Hektar zum Ziel und den Bau von zwei weiteren Startbahnen. Den Landesvätern schwebte damals ein Interkontinentalflughafen vor.

The story of resistance to the trade fair centre can be told from at least three different viewpoints. On the one hand, there are people such as Karl Kizele and Walter Stäbler who were directly affected by it. They fought against the hugely expensive exhibition complex for so many years because it constituted a threat to their very means of earning a living. For farmers like these, what happened with the trade fair centre was an experience fraught with drama. And like almost all dramas, this one started with a love affair. In this case, a love affair with the land.

But the story about the resistance could also be started with Leinfelden-Echterdingen, a town which is sometimes reminiscent of that small encircled village in Gaul which defends itself against overwhelming odds, against the failure of the Gallic capital to understand its problems and against interference in the planning sovereignty of the local community. A comparison with the village in Gaul is all the more appropriate given that the Ehapa Verlag publishing company, which was made rich by Asterix the Gaul, used to have a large office in this very town. Subsequently, Ehapa moved to Berlin, leaving Leinfelden-Echterdingen in a state of siege. The 36,000 inhabitants in the town opposed the trade fair centre vehemently and were quite prepared to put their money on the line in support of their stance. Although they spent more than 2.5 million euros on diverse campaigns, experts' assessments and lawyers, all their efforts and tribuluations turned out to have been in vain.

Finally, there is the third point of view. The story of the resistance could also be tied to the Filder area itself which had been targeted by the planners long before there were any thoughts of a new trade fair centre for Baden-Württemberg. This would seem to be the best approach given that the issues are more complicated than they appear to be to a lot of people and that anyone who lives there has had and is still having to cope with many problems associated with the merciless structural

Seite 040
Zeitweise bis zu 10.000 Filderbewohner unterstützten
in den vergangenen Jahrzehnten die Bürgerinitiative gegen
den Ausverkauf des Grüns auf den Fildern

Page 040
Inhabitants of the Filder area, sometimes up to 10,000
people, supported the citizens' initiative against the sale of
green fields in the Filder area in recent decades

Unter dem Protest der Bürgerinitiative, die in ihren besten Zeiten rund 10.000 Mitglieder zählte und in den achtziger Jahren mehr als 82.000 Einwendungen gegen den Flughafenausbau gesammelt hatte, wurden die Pläne für das umstrittene Großprojekt zumindest abgespeckt. Am Ende ist die Startbahn »nur« auf 3345 Meter verlängert worden. Das bis heute geltende Nachtflugverbot war ein weiteres Zugeständnis an die Gegner. Ihre Wunden hat das nicht geheilt.

Hier ist eine erste Zwischenbemerkung über die Standfestigkeit handelnder Personen fällig. Sie ist nötig, um den Zorn der Widerständler besser verstehen zu können. Dieser Zorn hat seine Wurzeln in der Geschichte politischer Gelübde, die auf den Fildern seit je von äußerst begrenzter Haltbarkeit waren. Bereits zu Beginn der sechziger Jahre hatte Stuttgarts damaliger Oberbürgermeister Arnulf Klett versprochen, jetzt sei Schluss mit dem Betonieren auf den Feldern im grünen Winkel zwischen Autobahn und Flughafen. Die Startbahn des Airports war gerade unter Protest von 1800 auf 2250 Meter verlängert worden. Klett sollte sich täuschen – und viele sahen sich getäuscht.

Kaum war dieses Versprechen gegeben, schwappte die Reisewelle bis nach Echterdingen. Es ging aufwärts in der Republik und bald regierte Ministerpräsident Lothar Späth das Land, der dem Wachstum das Wort redete. Wieder wurden den Landwirten viele Äcker abgetrotzt, wieder gab es eine Flurbereinigung und wieder sollte es das letzte Mal sein. Jedenfalls hat das Lothar Späth versprochen. Aber noch während Anfang der neunziger Jahre die Betonmischer rotierten und die Landebahn um einen weiteren Kilometer verlängert wurde, tauchte schon das nächste Projekt am Horizont des Landstrichs auf: Eine 100 Hektar große Messe sollte neben dem Flughafen entstehen. Späth wurde von Erwin Teufel abgelöst, der sich an das Wort seines Amtsvorgängers nicht gebunden fühlte. Abermals sahen sich viele getäuscht.

changes to which the Stuttgart conurbation has been and still is being subjected. Many of them have joined the Filder »Schutzgemeinschaft« (society for the protection of the Filder area). One of the oldest citizens' initiatives in Germany, it resists the modern urge to expand and the unrestrained appetite for more and more farmland. This appetite was stimulated a long time before any plans were drawn up for the trade fair centre but, in 1967, it became ravenous. At the time, the Gerlach plan was being considered by the state government. Its aim was to increase the size of the airport at Echterdingen from 272 to 1000 hectares and build two additional runways as well. Politicians were playing with the idea of creating an intercontinental airport for the area.

In the face of protests from the citizen's initiative, which counted 10,000 members in its best times and, in the 1980s, had collected more than 82,000 objections to the airport expansion, the plans for the controversial project were at least trimmed back. In the end, the length of the takeoff runway was »only« increased to 3345 metres. The prohibition on night flights, which is still in force today, was another concession to the opponents but it did not entirely heal their wounds.

At this point, it is worth commenting on the determination of the people involved in order to better understand the anger of the resisters at the time. It has its roots in the history of political promises, which have always had an extremely limited sell-by date when it comes to the Filder area. At the beginning of the 1960s, Stuttgart's lord mayor at the time, Arnulf Klett, promised to put a stop to construction in the Filder area in the green angle between the motorway and the airport. The take-off runway of the airport had just been lengthened from 1800 to 2250 metres against the protests of the locals. In the end, Klett was to be wrong-footed and many people felt deceived.

Der Widerstand der Filderbewohner artikulierte
sich auch in nächtlichen Protestmärschen

The resistance of the inhabitants of the Filder area
also expressed itself in protest marches at night

Scheckbuchpolitik und runde Tische

Dabei waren die ersten Anzeichen für einen neuerlichen Konflikt zwischen
Tradition und Moderne, zwischen Landwirtschaft und Standortpolitik, zwischen
Grundsätzen und Umsätzen in jener Zeit längst nicht mehr zu verkennen. Die
Stuttgarter FDP hatte den Stein ins Wasser geworfen und dafür geworben, den
Messestandort auf dem Killesberg aufzugeben. Unter diesen Vorzeichen ist
1992 die Weidleplan Consulting GmbH beauftragt worden, nach einem geeigneten
Standort für die neue Messe zu suchen. Nach Auswertung aller Suchschleifen
empfahlen die Gutachter »den Standort Echterdinger Ei-Ost«. Um das Vorhaben
juristisch und planerisch wasserdicht zu machen, lief in Baden-Württemberg
die bürokratische Maschinerie an. Das Landesmessegesetz wurde vorbereitet,
das die Notwendigkeit eines neuen Schaufensters für die Wirtschaft des Landes
unterstreicht. Der Verband Region Stuttgart legte den Standort für das Großprojekt im Regionalplan präzise fest und das Stuttgarter Regierungspräsidium
machte sich daran, die Argumente für und wider die neue Messe abzuwägen.
Auch die Schutzgemeinschaft bereitete sich vor und mobilisierte ihre Anhänger.
Rund um den geplanten Standort wurden Plakate aufgestellt. »Unsere Vorfahren
würden sich im Grab rumdrehen, müssten sie die Planungen auf den Fildern
sehen«, lautete die Botschaft.

An der Spitze der Messegegner standen sechs Bauern, denen per Ukas der
Landesregierung die Lebensgrundlage entzogen werden sollte. Nach den Plänen
für das Millionenprojekt hätten sie so viel Land verkaufen müssen, dass ihnen nur
unrentable Rumpfbetriebe geblieben wären. Es folgte eine lange Reihe recht-
licher und bürokratischer Verfahren. Zu den wichtigsten gehört die juristische Aus-
einandersetzung vor dem Bundesverwaltungsgericht in Leipzig. Dorthin hatte
sich die Stadt Leinfelden-Echterdingen durchgeklagt, die sich gegen den im Regionalplan ausgewiesenen Messeplatz vor ihren Toren wehrte. Die Richter ließen
die Stadt abblitzen und bestätigten die Pläne des Verbands Region Stuttgart.
Damit war der Standort für die neue Landesmesse zementiert.

Hardly had this promise been given when the
growing urge to travel to far-off places finally arrived at
Echterdingen. Things were going well in the republic and
soon Minister President Lothar Späth, for whom growth
was a magic word, ruled the state. Once again, the farmers
were compelled to give up large swathes of land, once
again agricultural land was reallocated and once again it
was to be the very last time. At least, this is what Lothar
Späth had vowed. Yet, hardly had the 1990s begun when
the concrete mixers started to rotate again and another
kilometre was added to the landing runway at the airport.
Soon after, the next project appeared on the horizon:
a 100 hectare trade fair centre was to be built next to the
airport. Späth was succeeded by Erwin Teufel, who did
not feel tied to the word of his predecessor. For the ump-
teenth time, people felt they had been given the run-
around.

Cheque-book politics and round tables

The first signs of a new conflict between tradition and
modernity, between agriculture and local politics, between
principles and money could no longer be ignored. The
Stuttgart branch of the FDP (free democratic party) had
set the ball rolling, advocating abandonment of the
Killesberg location as the venue for trade fairs. Against
this background, Weidleplan Consulting GmbH was
engaged in 1992 to look for a suitable location for the new
trade fair grounds. After evaluation of all the possible
sites turned up by the search, the experts recommended
the »Echterdinger Ei-Ost« (the Echterdingen egg east)
location. In order to make the plan water-tight from a legal
and planning point of view, the bureaucratic machinery in
Baden-Württemberg was set in motion. Subsequently,
the state trade fair law was drafted and underlined the ne-
cessity for a new showcase that would be able to present
the state's industry and commerce. The Verband Region
Stuttgart (association for the promotion of Stuttgart
as a region) precisely defined the location for the large-
scale project in the plan for the region and Stuttgart's
governing body began to consider the pros and cons of the
new trade fair venue. The »Schutzgemeinschaft« also
made its preparations and began to mobilize its support-
ers. All round the planned site, posters were erected.
»Our ancestors would turn in their graves if they saw the
plans for the Filder area« was the message.

Eine Sitzblockade der Messegegner verzögerte
den Baubeginn um einige Tage

A sit-in of opponents of the trade fair centre cause the
start of construction to be delayed by several days

Nach diesem Urteil verkauften viele Grundstücksbesitzer, die noch gezö-
gert hatten, ihre Parzellen an das Land. Umso mehr ruhten die letzten Hoffnungen
der Widerständler auf den sechs Bauern, die bereit waren, alle juristischen
Mittel auszuschöpfen. Den Streitparteien stand ein langer Weg durch die Instanzen bevor, was vor allem die Landesregierung vor Probleme stellte. Der Bau
drohte sich zu verteuern, die Stuttgarter Messegesellschaft sah auf dem hart um-
kämpften Ausstellungsmarkt ihre Felle davonschwimmen. Es folgte die hohe
Zeit der Scheckbuchpolitik und der runden Tische, um das eckige Problem zu lösen.
Ministerpräsident Erwin Teufel stellte der Stadt Leinfelden-Echterdingen im
Januar 2004 eine stolze Entschädigung in Aussicht, wenn sie ihren Widerstand
gegen die Messe aufgibt und die anhängige Klage gegen den zwischenzeitlich
ergangenen Baubeschluss zurücknimmt. Dafür winkten der Stadt für eine Stadt-
bahnverlängerung und für Lärmschutz erkleckliche Zuschüsse, die sich auf
35 Millionen summiert hätten. Doch der Gemeinderat erlag dieser Versuchung
nicht. Die Stadt zahlte dafür einen hohen Preis. Sie verlor vor Gericht und stand
am Ende mit leeren Händen da.

Der Durchbruch
Auch Landwirte wie Karl Kizele und Walter Stäbler wurden kräftig »massiert«,
wie das im Jargon der Politik heißt. Die klagenden Bauern bekamen attraktive
Höfe angeboten, in Gegenden, in denen die Natur noch mit breitem Strich aufge-
tragen ist. Es waren verlockende Offerten darunter, aber die Berufskollegen
hatten sich versprochen, mit offenen Karten zu spielen und gemeinsam bis zum
Ende zu kämpfen. Für sie ging es um Millionen. Das Land bot 53 Euro pro Quadratmeter, wenn sie freiwillig verkaufen – und es drohte mit der Enteignung, wenn
sie nicht verkaufen. In diesem Fall hätten die Bauern für ihre Äcker weniger als
die Hälfte bekommen. Durch manche Familien ging ein Riss. Aber noch standen
die Landwirte fest zusammen, angeführt vom Echterdinger Rebellen Walter
Stäbler, der sich am lautesten gegen die Messe wehrte und die Filder bei allfälli-
ger Gelegenheit als »das Paradies« bezeichnete.

The opposition to the trade fair was headed by six
farmers, whose livelihood was to be taken away by the
state government by decree. According to the plans for the
extremely costly project, they would have had to sell so
much land that they would only have been left with un-
profitable »rump« farms. There followed a long series of
legal and bureaucratic conflicts. Among the most important was the legal dispute before the Federal Administrative Court in Leipzig. The Leinfelden-Echterdingen
municipal authorities that were against the trade fair site
allocated in the plan for the region had managed to
bring their case so far. However, the judges dismissed their
appeal and confirmed the plans of the Verband Region
Stuttgart. The location for the new state trade fair centre
was thus decided on once and for all.

After this judgement, many landowners who
had hesitated up to that moment sold their land to the
state. This was all the more reason for the resistance
campaign to place its last hopes on the six farmers who
were prepared to exhaust all the legal pathways. The
disputing parties were faced with a long haul through the
various courts and this made life difficult, especially for
the state government. The construction costs threatened
to soar and the Stuttgart trade fair company saw its
chances in the highly competitive exhibition market slowly
trickling away. It was then that the time of cheque-book
politics and round tables arrived in order to solve the
tricky problem that somehow had to be dealt with. In January 2004, Minister President Erwin Teufel offered a large
sum in compensation to Leinfelden-Echterdingen if it
gave up its resistance to the trade fair centre and withdrew
its pending legal case against the construction plan,
which had been ratified in the meantime. The town stood
to gain considerable grants totalling EUR 35 million for
an extension of the rapid transit line and for noise protection structures. But, the local council did not succumb
to this temptation. In the end, it paid a high price for its
refusal – it lost its case before the courts and was left
empty-handed.

An dieser Stelle ist die nächste Bemerkung zur Standfestigkeit fällig. Ausgerechnet Frontmann Stäbler wurde plötzlich schwach. Hinter dem Rücken seiner ahnungslosen Mitstreiter verhandelte er mit der Landsiedlung Baden-Württemberg, verkaufte seine Äcker und tauschte seinen umzingelten Betrieb in Echterdingen gegen einen riesigen Hof am Bodensee ein. Es war das Geschäft seines Lebens. Der Lockruf des Geldes war stärker als die innere Überzeugung, den Kampf gegen die Messe noch auf juristischem Wege gewinnen zu können, nachdem alle Klagen bisher in den ersten Instanzen gescheitert waren.

Dies war der eigentliche Durchbruch für die Messe. Am 4. August 2004 wurde der Handel in der Villa Reitzenstein besiegelt. Die Bauern bekamen den Höchstpreis für ihre Äcker und verpflichteten sich im Gegenzug, nicht weiter gegen das Projekt zu klagen. Von dem Geld aus dem Verkauf ihrer Grundstücke konnten sie die Äcker des abgewanderten Kollegen Stäbler erwerben. Darüber hinaus versprach das Land, zusätzlich 50 Hektar Pachtland aufzutreiben, damit alle Betriebe dauerhaft gesichert werden können. Die Landwirte mussten dafür ihrerseits versprechen, die nächste Stufe der Expansion nicht zu torpedieren. Sie verpflichteten sich, auch jene Felder zu verkaufen, die für eine geplante Westerweiterung des Flughafens benötigt werden. Und so ist es auch gekommen.

Es sollte nicht lange dauern, bis sich viele der Widerständler mit der neuen Situation arrangierten. Im Gästebuch auf der Messebaustelle tauchten bereits nach wenigen Monaten immer öfter Namen auf, die in der Vergangenheit mit dem

The breakthrough

Farmers such as Karl Kizele and Walter Stäbler were also given a good »going-over«. They were offered attractive farms in districts where the natural surroundings were still largely untouched. Some of the offers were extremely tempting but the farmers had promised each other to play with their cards on the table and fight the plans to the bitter end together. For them, sums amounting to millions of euros were involved. The state offered 53 euros per square meter if they sold voluntarily, and threatened them with expropriation if they refused to sell. In this case, the farmers would have received less than half of the land's worth. In many families, there was a split. But the farmers stood shoulder to shoulder, led by the Echterdingen rebel Walter Stäbler, who was the loudest opponent of the trade fair centre and described the Filder area as »paradise« whenever he had an opportunity to be heard.

Another comment on the determination of the resistance is worth making here. Front man Stäbler, of all people, suddenly began to weaken. Behind the backs of unsuspecting fellow objectors, he negotiated with the Landsiedlung (state land settlement body) of Baden-Württemberg, sold his land and exchanged his fenced-in farm in Echterdingen for a huge farm near Lake Constance. It was the best deal he ever made in his life. The enticement of money was stronger than the inner conviction of being able to win the struggle against the trade fair centre through legal channels after all the cases brought to court had failed on their first hearing.

This was the real breakthrough for the trade fair centre. On 4th August 2004, the seal was put on the transaction in Villa Reitzenstein. The farmers received the maximum price for their land and, in reciprocation, undertook not to pursue their case against the project in court. From the money received from the sale of their land, they were able to purchase the fields of their colleague Walter Stäbler, who had by now left the scene. The state also promised to come up with an additional 50 hectares of leased land so that all the farms could be safeguarded permanently. For their part, the farmers had to promise not to torpedo the next expansion phase. They also undertook to sell those fields which would be needed for a further airport expansion to the west. And this is what then happened.

Protest in Verbindung gebracht worden waren. Der Gemeinderat von Leinfelden-Echterdingen besuchte nicht nur die imposante Baustelle, sondern plante auch ein nicht minder imposantes Gewerbegebiet neben den Ausstellungshallen. Einige Bauern verdienten gutes Geld mit Zubringerdiensten zum Flughafen, indem sie Urlauber bei sich auf dem Hof parken ließen. Und der abtrünnige Landwirt Walter Stäbler hat sich schnell an sein Zuhause am Bodensee gewöhnt. Für ihn ist jetzt sein neuer Hof »das Paradies«.

Die dritte und letzte Bemerkung zur Standfestigkeit handelnder Personen weist in die Zukunft. Man muss kein Prophet sein, um vorherzusagen, dass es weitere Begehrlichkeiten geben wird. Noch während die Bagger über die Messebaustelle rollten, wurden die nächsten Pläne für die Aussaat von Beton auf den fruchtbaren Lösslehm-Böden der Filderebene ruchbar. Der Flughafendirektor Georg Fundel hat sie aus einer Schublade gezogen, wo sie auf Geheiß von Erwin Teufel über Jahre hinweg lagen. Der frühere Ministerpräsident hatte erkannt, dass eine öffentliche Debatte über solche Pläne zur falschen Zeit nicht nur die Messe gefährden, sondern auch das Fass rund um Echterdingen zum Überlaufen bringen könnten. Inzwischen allerdings verzeichnet der Flughafen jährlich neue Passagierrekorde, die Kapazitätsgrenze von 180.000 Starts und Landungen im Jahr dürfte spätestens 2014 erreicht sein. Die Schlüsse aus diesen Zahlen sind klar: Eine zweite Startbahn soll gebaut werden. Sie wird das Feuer des Widerstands neu entfachen.

It was not to be long before many of the trade fair opponents came to terms with the situation. In the visitors' book at the construction site for the centre, names which had earlier been associated with protests began to appear with increasing regularity. The municipal council of Leinfelden-Echterdingen not only visited the highly impressive building site but also planned to create a no less impressive industrial park near the exhibition halls. Some farmers earned good money with transit services to the airport, allowing holidaymakers to park on their land. As for the renegade farmer Walter Stäbler, he soon got used to his new home next to Lake Constance. For him, his new farm is now his new »paradise«.

A third and last comment on the determination of the people involved is a pointer for the future. It is not necessary to be a clairvoyant to know that there will be further instances of covetousness in the future. Even as the excavators were rolling over the building site for the trade fair centre, the next plans for spreading concrete over the fertile loess and clay soil of the Filder fields were looming. Airport director Georg Fundel took them out of a drawer where they had rested for many years at the bidding of Erwin Teufel. The former minister president had known that a public debate on such plans – if initiated at the wrong time – would not only have endangered the trade fair project but could also have been the last straw for Echterdingen. In the meantime, however, the airport is enjoying record numbers of passengers year after year. The capacity limit of 180,000 take-offs and landings per year will probably be reached by 2014 at the latest. The conclusions to be drawn from these figures is clear: a second take-off runway will be needed. There should be no surprise if this re-ignites the hot flame of resistance.

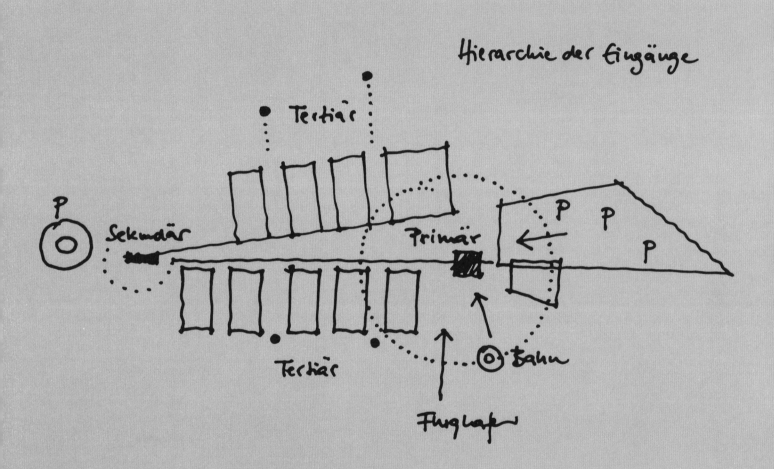

Hierarchie der Eingänge

P

Tertiär

Sekundär

Primär

P P

P

Tertiär

Bahn

Flughafen

Die Messe in der Landschaft

Tobias Wulf
vom Architekturbüro
Wulf & Partner im
Gespräch mit Falk Jaeger

Trade fair centre in the landscape

Tobias Wulf
from architect's office
Wulf & Partner
talking to Falk Jaeger

Die Messe
in der Landschaft
Tobias Wulf
vom Architekturbüro
Wulf & Partner im
Gespräch mit Falk Jaeger

Trade fair centre in
the landscape
Tobias Wulf
from architect's office
Wulf & Partner
talking to Falk Jaeger

FJ   Wie geht man eine solch herkulische Aufgabe an, eine Messe zu planen? Wie kommt man zu ersten Ideenskizzen?

TW   Mit einer Skizze fing es eigentlich nicht an. Eher mit einem Lernprozess, nachdem wir uns dazu durchgerungen hatten, an diesem Wettbewerb teilzunehmen. Während der ersten Woche haben wir den umfangreichen Auslobungstext durchgearbeitet, der eher einem dicken Buch ähnelt, vollgepackt mit Informationen. Es hat gedauert, bis das alles einigermaßen im Kopf war. Wir waren damals Neulinge auf dem Gebiet des Messebaus und wussten, wie politisch umstritten diese große Bauaufgabe war. Anfangs war uns noch nicht klar, wie wir uns positionieren sollten. Wir haben uns zusammengesetzt und gemeinsam Ideen entwickelt, die von politischen Ideologien unabhängig waren. In dieser Phase war der Landschaftsplaner bereits beteiligt.

FJ   Wie haben sich diese Ideen dann konkretisiert?

TW   Wir haben ein Modell im Maßstab 1:2000 gebaut und gleichzeitig viel skizziert. Schließlich hatten wir mehrere für uns wichtige Aspekte herausgearbeitet. Einer davon war die Frage, wie man diese Messe so gestalten kann, dass sie sich vom internationalen Messeeinerlei unterscheidet. Messeplanung wird in der Regel nicht als Architekturthema gesehen, sondern eher als möglichst rasche Produktion möglichst großer Ausstellungsflächen. So wollten wir an das Thema natürlich nicht herangehen. Dazu kam ein zweiter entscheidender Punkt, nämlich das Gelände. Wir finden hier kein ideales, ebenes Gelände vor, sondern nach Osten ein leichtes Gefälle von 20 Metern. Uns war bald klar, dass dieses Gelände eine große Herausforderung war, weil wir es nicht einebnen konnten. Also entschlossen wir uns dazu, Höhenstufen einzuführen. Eine der wesentlichen Ideen war also, dass man nicht nur im Grundriss entwirft, sondern auch im Schnitt, was ungewöhnlich ist für eine Messe. Die dritte große Maxime war für uns, möglichst wenig Fläche zu verbrauchen, also möglichst nah am Flughafen zu bleiben.

FJ   How did you approach such a herculean task as planning a trade fair centre? How did you arrive at the initial sketch of an idea?

TW   It did not actually begin with a sketch. Rather with a process of learning after we had finally convinced ourselves that it was worth taking part in this competition. During the first week, we worked through the extensive specifications in the text of the invitation. It was more like a thick book than a simple invitation and was packed full of information. It took us some time before we had a good idea of what was required of us. At the time, we were novices in the field of trade fair construction but were aware of just how politically controversial this large project was. We were not sure what approach we should adopt in the beginning so we sat down together and developed some ideas which were independent of any particular political ideology. In this phase, the landscape planner was already involved.

FJ   How were these ideas then given concrete form?

TW   We built a model on a scale of 1:2000 and, at the same time, prepared a great many sketches. In the end, we had worked out several important aspects which were important for us. One was the question as to how the trade fair centre could be designed in such a way that it would stand out from the usual trade fair monotony to be found practically everywhere else in the country. Trade fair planning is not usually seen as an architectural issue. It tends to require the fastest possible creation of the largest possible exhibition areas so we naturally did not want to go in that direction. There was also another decisive point: the site that had been chosen. The terrain was not ideal and even but had a slight slope of 20 metres towards the east. It soon became clear to us that this terrain was a huge challenge because we couldn't level it out. So we decided to use terraces. One of the fundamental ideas was to design not only on the plane of the ground plan but also with staggered heights. This is unusual for a trade fair site, to say the least. Our third main aim was to use as little space as possible, in other words to stay as close to the airport as possible.

FJ Schon der Testentwurf der Ausschreibung widersprach allerdings diesen Maximen.

TW Ja, das war gewissermaßen schon die nächste Mutprobe. Natürlich bot es sich zunächst an, sich an diesem Testentwurf zu orientieren. Aber es liegt nun einmal in der Natur unseres Büros, immer etwas quer zu denken und einen besseren Ansatz finden zu wollen als das Naheliegende.

FJ Wie gingen Sie mit dem Problem Flächenverbrauch um?

TW Wir haben die Bauten möglichst eng an den Flughafen gelegt und damit eben nicht, wie im Testentwurf vorgesehen, parallel zur Autobahn, sondern parallel zum Flughafen. Auf diese Weise haben wir erreicht, dass keine Leerfläche zwischen Flughafen und Messe entsteht und dass wir nur eine einzige Bebauungsinsel auf den Fildern haben.

Dazu kam die Entscheidung, das Parkhaus über die Autobahn zu legen. Dieser Schritt lag nicht unbedingt nahe, weil er teure Konstruktionen nach sich zieht, aber für uns war der geringere Flächenverbrauch wichtiger. Ökonomie muss sich nicht unbedingt in Kostenzahlen ausdrücken.

Man kann auch sagen, wir haben einen ökologischen Ansatz verfolgt. Natürlich muss man dies durch Anführungszeichen relativieren, aber wir haben zum Beispiel die Dächer der Messehallen teilweise begrünt, ebenso das Parkhaus. So etwas trifft man normalerweise bei Messen nicht an. Die Frage des Landschaftsverbrauchs war aber auch als politisches Argument gegenüber der skeptischen Bevölkerung sehr wichtig. Und es war uns wichtig, dass sich die Besucher auf diesem großen Areal gut orientieren können. Daher galt es, Monotonie und Symmetrien ebenso wie Wiederholungen zu vermeiden, weil das die Orientierung erschwert. Aus diesem Grund haben wir die Mittelachse leicht geöffnet, sodass die Messehallen sich nicht parallel gegenüberstehen, sondern etwas verschwenkt.

FJ The test design in the invitation to take part contradicted all of these aims.

TW Yes, that was, so to say, the first challenge we were confronted with. Initially, of course, it was tempting to keep to this test design. But, lateral thinking is in the nature of our office and we always like to find a better approach than the most obvious one that presents itself.

FJ How did you handle the problem of the amount of space that would be needed?

TW We placed the buildings as close to the airport as possible and, in contrast to the test design, not parallel to the motorway but parallel to the airport. In this way, we ensured that there was no empty space between the airport and the trade fair site and that we only had one single »island« for building in the Filder area.

Then, there was the decision to build the multi-storey car park over the motorway. This was not something we necessarily wanted to do because it involved additional expense with regard to the technical construction. But for us, using less space was a more important consideration. Economy does not necessarily have to be expressed in terms of cost.

You could also say that we adopted an ecological approach. Of course, this must be relativised with quotation marks around this statement but, for example, we planned to landscape some of the roofs of the trade fair halls and the top of the multi-storey car park as well. This is not normally done with trade fair installations. The question of land use, however, was also a political question in view of the scepticism exhibited by the local population. It was also important for us to make sure that visitors would be easily able to find their way about this very large site. We therefore aimed at reducing monotony, symmetry and a repetition of structures as they tend to make orientation very difficult. This is why we slightly opened the middle axis so that the trade fair halls were not parallel to each other but were slightly divergent.

FJ   Ergab sich die Stellung der Hallen quer zum Hang gestaffelt automatisch aus der Hanglage?

TW   Ja, wobei das Gefälle genauso in der anderen Richtung vorhanden gewesen wäre. Auch die Konkurrenzentwürfe haben sich mit dem Problem der Niveauunterschiede auseinandergesetzt und dies meist durch eine riesige Treppenanlage am Anfang bewältigt, die man hätte überwinden müssen.

FJ   Und die liegt bei Ihrem Entwurf sozusagen intern.

TW   In der Terrassierung. Die Architekten in der Jury haben das sofort verstanden, während die Messefachleute zunächst nicht dreidimensional dachten und davon ausgingen, dass die Besucher ständig die Ebenen wechseln müssten. Für uns war der Vorteil entscheidend, dass wir durch diese drei Geländestufen Querverbindungen zwischen den einzelnen Zulieferhöfen herstellen können und daher keine äußere Messeumfahrung notwendig ist. Die Zulieferer haben also kürzere Wege. Dieses überzeugende funktionale Argument ergab sich aus unserer Landschaftsidee.

Unser Entwurf folgt nicht ausschließlich funktionalen Erfordernissen – diese zu erfüllen muss selbstverständlich sein –, sondern er entstand im Wesentlichen aus übergeordneten Kriterien der Landschaft und der Wahrnehmung von Raum. Wir haben zum Beispiel analysiert, wie die Gewässer auf den Fildern laufen, nämlich hauptsächlich in West-Ost-Richtung. Auch die Besiedlungsstruktur hat sich in dieser Richtung entwickelt. Es ist also kein Zufall, wenn wir genau diese Richtung wieder aufgenommen haben. Eher zufällig hat sich ergeben, dass die Messeachse genau auf der Verbindungslinie der Kirchtürme von Plieningen und Echterdingen liegt – für mich eine gewisse Bestätigung, dass dieser Gedanke nicht so ganz falsch war.

FJ   Was the position of the halls transversely to the slope and in a staggered layout an automatic result of the location on an incline?

TW   Yes, although the slope would have been present in the other direction as well. The rival designs also considered the problem of level differences, mostly by envisaging a huge staircase that people would have had to climb.

FJ   And this is internal, as it were, to your design.

TW   In the terracing. The architects on the jury understood this immediately whereas, at the outset, the trade fair specialists did not think three-dimensionally and assumed that visitors would have to change continually from one level to the next. For us, one advantage was crucial, namely that, as a result of the three terraces, cross-connections between the individual delivery yards could be established and it would not be necessary to drive around the trade fair outside the actual site. The distances for suppliers were therefore shorter. This convincing functional argument resulted from our landscaping idea.

Our design did not seek to meet only functional requirements – fulfilling them is a given – but was mainly the consequence of superordinate criteria regarding the landscape and the perception of space. For example, we analysed the course of the waterways in the Filder area, namely in a west-east direction. Residential development had also progressed in this direction. It was therefore no coincidence that we adopted precisely this direction again. It is more a matter of chance, however, that the axis of the trade fair site is exactly on a line between the church towers of Plieningen and Echterdingen – for me, a kind of confirmation that this idea was not completely wrong.

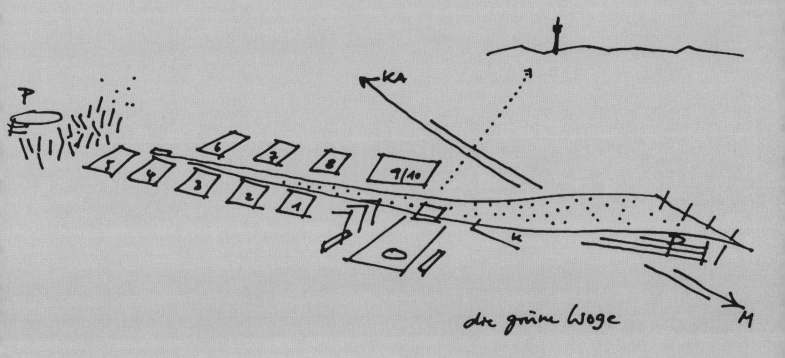

FJ   Wie kam es zu der ungewöhnlichen Form der Hallen mit ihren Hängedächern?

TW   Ein zugbeanspruchtes Hängedach ist eine spannende Bauweise. Uns hat das aber, das muss man klar sagen, nicht nur von der Konstruktion her interessiert, sondern auch von der Form. Denn diese Form gibt der Messe etwas Unverwechselbares und fügt sich unserer Meinung nach sehr gut in die hügelige Voralblandschaft ein. Ich muss dazu sagen, dass wir nicht nur den Landschaftsplaner mit im Team hatten, sondern auch den Tragwerksplaner, mit dem wir die Konstruktion dieser ausdrucksstarken Form weiterentwickelt haben.

FJ   Wie legitimiert sich das verhältnismäßig teure Parkhaus?

TW   Neben der guten Flächenökonomie, die sich durch die Doppelbelegung des Areals ergibt – also Parkhaus und Autobahn –, spielt die Aussicht vom Dach des Parkhauses eine wichtige Rolle. Von hier aus sieht man auf das Flugfeld und hat ebenso wie vom Messevorplatz den Stuttgarter Fernsehturm im Blick. Dieser Sichtbezug zum Fernsehturm war uns wichtig. Als Messebesucher spürt man so auch außerhalb der Stadt, dass man sich in Stuttgart befindet. Der Fernsehturm ist das Wahrzeichen der Stadt und stellt den Bezug zum Ort her. Wichtig ist auch, dass der Brückenbau über der Autobahn nach außen hin für täglich Tausende von Autofahrern als starkes Zeichen wirkt.

Auch funktionale Vorteile sprechen für diese Parkhauslösung, etwa die Erschließung von beiden Seiten der Autobahn aus oder die Brückenfunktion durch den Fußweg, auf dem man von der Plieninger Seite aus zum Flughafen gelangen kann. Außerdem liegt das Parkhaus nicht nur sehr günstig zum Haupteingang der Messe, sondern auch zum Flughafen. Es wird zum Beispiel im Sommer, wenn während der Hauptreisezeit in der Messe wenig Betrieb ist, hauptsächlich von Flughafengästen benutzt. Deshalb hat sich die Flughafengesellschaft bereit erklärt, die Bauherrschaft zu übernehmen und das Parkhaus zu finanzieren.

FJ   How did you arrive at the unusual shape of the halls and their suspended roofs?

TW   A suspended roof subjected to tensile force is an exciting form of construction. But, it must be said, this not only interested us in terms of its technical aspects but also in respect of its shape and appearance. The reason is that the shape gives the trade fair centre something unique and, in our opinion, fits very well into the hilly landscape of the area. One other thing I must say is that we not only had a landscape planner in the team but also a structural engineer who helped us to refine the technical aspects of this highly expressive shape.

FJ   How is the relatively expensive multi-storey car park justified?

TW   Apart from the good economics of space resulting from dual use of the area – i.e. multi-storey car park and motorway –, the view from the roof of the multi-storey car park played a fairly important role. From here, you can see the airfield and the Stuttgart television tower, which is also visible from the forecourt of the trade fair centre. This visible relationship to the television tower was important for us. Trade fair visitors will have the feeling of being in Stuttgart even though they are actually outside the city. After all, the television tower is the landmark of the city and, to some extent, represents the location and the region. It is also important that the bridge built over the motorway is a powerful sign for the thousands of car drivers who use the motorway every day.

Functional advantages also speak in favour of this multi-storey car park solution such as access to the trade fair centre from both sides of the motorway or on foot over the bridge which can be used to get from the Plieningen side to the airport. Apart from this, the multi-storey car park is not only very favourably placed in relation to the trade fair entrance but also in respect of getting to the airport. In summer, for example, when not much will be happening in the trade fair centre as it is the main holiday period, it will primarily be used by airline passengers with cars. This is why the airport company agreed to act as the client and finance the multi-storey car park.

FJ Der Durchblick zwischen den beiden Parkhausflügeln ist die Verlängerung der grünen Messeachse. Welche Funktion hat diese Achse? Soll sie Ausstellern und Besuchern Erholung bieten?

TW Etwas überspitzt gesagt, ist das der Central Park der Messe. Die Besucher gehen in diesen Park, um sich zu entspannen. Etwas Grün, frische Luft und Erholung von der Reizüberflutung in den Messehallen, so wird man den Park erleben.

FJ Wie kann man eine Messe stilistisch, semantisch in architektonische Formen fassen? Haben Sie Ihre charakteristische Architektursprache eingesetzt oder versucht, ein spezifisches Vokabular zu finden?

TW Zunächst einmal ist der Messehallenbau ein eher architekturfeindliches Thema, weil es ausschließlich darum geht, möglichst flexible, am besten überhaupt nicht mit Tageslicht versehene Ausstellungsfläche bereitzustellen. Ein solcher Bau lebt ausschließlich innen, die äußere Hülle ist kaum mehr als ein notwendiges Übel. Genau so sehen viele Messen auch aus. Für uns war es wichtig, wie die Bauten von außen wirken. Sie müssen innen funktionieren, das ist klar, aber der Raum muss von außen und innen mehr sein als nur ein gesichtsloser Container. Als wir uns umgesehen haben, entdeckten wir auch Messehallen, die mit Tageslicht funktionieren und mit besonderen Konstruktionen ungewöhnliche Formen zeigen, wie zum Beispiel die Messehalle 26 in Hannover. Wir haben versucht, das Thema des Hängedachs weiterzuentwickeln.

Besonders spannend wird das bei der Hochhalle, wo wir zwei Standardhallen gegeneinander gestellt haben und in der Silhouette eine zirkuszeltartige Form entsteht. Hier haben wir eine besonders spezifische Architektursprache eingesetzt, die das Bild der Messe prägen wird.

FJ The view between the two wings of the multi-storey car park reveals the extension of the green trade fair axis. What function does this axis have? Is it somewhere for exhibitors and visitors to take a rest?

TW To put it in somewhat exaggerated terms, it is the Central Park of the trade fair centre. Visitors go into this park to relax. A landscaped environment, fresh air and an opportunity to recover from the flood of impressions absorbed in the trade fair halls – this is what the park will mean.

FJ How can a trade fair centre be stylistically and semantically interpreted in architectural terms? Did you use your characteristic architectural language or did you try to develop a specific vocabulary?

TW First of all, the construction of trade fair halls tends to be inimical to the idea of architecture as such because the only concern is to provide an exhibition space which is as flexible as possible and preferably is not exposed to daylight at all. Such a building only lives on the inside; the outer shell is hardly more than a necessary evil. And this is exactly what many trade fair centres look like. For us, what the buildings looked like on the outside was an extremely important issue. They have to function on the inside, of course, but, on the outside and inside, should be more than merely faceless containers. When we looked around, we also found trade fair halls which not only worked with daylight but also had special technical aspects with unusual shapes and forms. Trade fair hall number 26 in Hanover, for example. Our aim in this case was to improvise on the idea of the suspended roof.

This is especially exciting in the case of the high hall, where we have placed two standard halls opposite each other to produce a silhouette which is very similar to that of a circus tent. Here, we made use of a special architectural language which will finally determine the image of the trade fair centre as a whole.

00 – 07
**Der lange Weg
vom ersten Spatenstich
zur Einweihung**
Kai Bierich
vom Architekturbüro
Wulf & Partner

00 – 07
**The long way from
the first cut of the spade
to inauguration**
Kai Bierich
from architect's office
Wulf & Partner

00 – 07
Der lange Weg
vom ersten Spatenstich
zur Einweihung
Kai Bierich
vom Architekturbüro
Wulf & Partner

00 – 07
The long way from
the first cut of the spade
to inauguration
Kai Bierich
from architect's office
Wulf & Partner

Selten erleben wir, dass Visionen wahr werden. Die Schwierigkeiten bei der Grenzwanderung zwischen der Vision und den Möglichkeiten der Realisierung beschreibt der deutsche Philosoph und Hauptvertreter des Idealismus Georg Wilhelm Friedrich Hegel mit den Worten »Erst die Wahrheit einer Absicht ist die Tat«. Will sagen: Erst die Umsetzung bestätigt den Gehalt der Vision. Hegels Philosophie gilt nun als eine der komplexesten in der Philosophiegeschichte und rückt gerade daher in inhaltliche Nähe zur Umsetzung dieses ebenso idealistisch wie komplex angegangenen Großprojekts.

Denn gleichermaßen für Architekten wie für die Architektur ist der Sprung von mittleren Projekten zu einem Vorhaben dieser Größenordnung gewaltig. Dieser »große Sprung nach vorn« bezog sich hier auf alle Bereiche – verfahrensrechtliche, personelle, planerische und technische. Für alle Beteiligten wurde die Dimension des Projekts zu einer Herausforderung, die nur in sehr enger und professioneller Zusammenarbeit geleistet werden konnte.

Wie bei allen Großbauprojekten schob sich auch bei der Messe die Welt der Ingenieure und hier insbesondere das Thema der Konstruktion formal stark in den Vordergrund. So gut wie alle Bauteile der Messe sind von ihrer Konstruktion bestimmt. Bereits in der Wettbewerbsphase war daher eine enge Einbindung der Tragwerks-, Verkehrs-, Außenanlagen- und Infrastrukturplaner Voraussetzung sowohl für den Wettbewerbserfolg im Jahr 2000 als auch für die Fertigstellung bis 2007.

Politisches

Die politische Dimension war diesem Projekt, das von Stadt, Land und Region zugleich finanziert wird, allein durch die Größenordnung ein ständiger Begleiter. Die Folge war, dass sich im gesamten Verlauf sowohl Für- als auch genauso viele Gegensprecher zu Wort meldeten (und wieder verschwanden), um die Termine und Kosten, später auch Gestalt- und Materialideen immer wieder neu zu diskutieren. Es tauchten Vorschläge auf, wie man die Gesamtkosten halbieren könnte, wie man die Hallen in Holz konstruieren, eine Messe mittels eines Fertigteilsystems bauen oder – zumindest an manchen Stellen – den Willen zur Sparsamkeit demonstrieren könnte; Alltag eines Großprojekts.

It is a rare experience when we witness a vision coming true. The difficulties in moving over the line from vision to reality were described succinctly by Georg Wilhelm Friedrich Hegel. According to the German philosopher and main proponent of idealism, »only the deed itself constitutes the truth of the intention«. In other words, only concrete implementation confirms the content of the vision. Hegel's philosophy is now regarded as one of the most complex in the history of philosophy and, in respect of content, is a highly appropriate reference in any discussion of how this outstanding large-scale project, the lead-up to which was as idealistic as it was complex, was actually realised.

For architects and architecture, the leap from medium-sized projects to one of this size is enormous. In this case, the »great leap forward« was comprehensive and profound, encompassing legal procedures, personnel, planning and all the technical aspects. For all those involved, the dimensions of the project developed into a considerable challenge which could only be mastered through very close and committed professional collaboration.

As in all large-scale construction projects, the engineering of the trade fair centre, especially the aspect of structural engineering design, was a central formal focus. Practically all parts of the trade fair centre are dependent on their engineering design. As early as the competition phase, therefore, close involvement of the people responsible for the load-bearing structure, the traffic aspects, the outdoor installations and the infrastructure was a prerequisite for the success of the competition in 2000 and also for completion in 2007.

Political factors

Due to its sheer size, the political dimension was ever present in this project, which was co-financed by the city, the state and the region. The consequence was that, in the whole course of the project, those in favour and just as many opponents came forward to express their opinions (and then simply disappeared again). Deadlines and costs, as well as, later, ideas of design and materials, were brought to the discussion table again and again.

Kostenkontrollen und Einsparrunden wurden so zum ständigen Begleiter und schon in den ersten Wochen nach dem gewonnenen Wettbewerb wurden bei der Überarbeitung erhebliche Volumina eingespart. Durch die Verlegung einer der Messehallen aus der Südreihe in die Nordreihe und den Wegfall einer zweiten wurde es möglich, das Congresscenter vom Ostrand der Messeplaza an deren Westseite zu verschieben und damit an die Messehallen anzubinden. Dadurch ergaben sich erhebliche Vorteile bei den funktionalen Zusammenhängen zwischen Kongress und Messe. Zudem konnte die Klimazentrale in den Kongresskomplex integriert werden, wodurch nennenswerte Einsparungen bei Investitionen und Betriebskosten aufgrund der kürzeren Leitungswege ermöglicht wurden.

Der Öffnungswinkel des Freibereichs zwischen den beiden Hallenreihen wurde reduziert. Damit ergab sich eine deutliche Verschlankung der Eingangsbereiche. In diesem Zusammenhang wurde auch das Parkhaus mit seinen drei über die Autobahn reichenden Brücken auf zwei Finger vereinfacht, was weitere nennenswerte Einsparungen mit sich brachte.

Rechtliches

Erheblichen Widerstand und Konflikte gab es vor dem Hintergrund der drohenden Enteignungen der Landwirte sowie dem Eingriff in die kommunale Planungshoheit der betroffenen Gemeinden. Das durchgeführte Planfeststellungsverfahren, das sich in mehr als 180 Aktenordnern niederschlug, die öffentlichen Erörterungen und der ungewohnte Gegenwind wurden zur Nagelprobe für die neu zusammengewürfelte Planungsmannschaft.

In seinen Anforderungen an Umfang und Planungstiefe geht das Verfahren weit über die bewährte und geübte Praxis der Baugenehmigung hinaus und regelt sämtliche eingaberelevanten Aspekte in einem Zug. Die geforderte Bündelung der Belange Verkehr, Naturschutz, Ökologie, Brandschutz, Statik, Städtebau usw. verlangte den schnellen Aufbau eines schlagkräftigen und interdisziplinär arbeitenden Teams. Bereits in dieser frühen Phase ging es bei dem Verfahren um die gebietsscharfe Definition der Messe in Layout, Dimension und Proportion, die – später kaum mehr veränderbar – Grundlage für alle weiteren Planungen und Planer wurde.

There were proposals to halve the total costs, to make the halls out of wood, to build a trade fair centre with a system of prefabricated components or – at least in some cases – to demonstrate a willingness to be economical in thought and in deed. The everyday life of a large-scale project, in fact.

Cost monitoring and discussions on how to save money thus became constant companions and, even in the first weeks after the competition had been won, considerable volume savings were made during the design refinement process. One of the trade fair halls from the south row was moved into the north row, for example, while a second one was dispensed with altogether due to the revisions that were made. This made it possible to move the congress centre from its original location at the eastern edge of the trade fair plaza to its west side and thus link it up to the trade fair halls nearby. As a result, considerable advantages were gained in respect of the functional interrelationships that exist between congress and trade fair. In addition, it was possible to integrate the air-conditioning control centre in the congress complex, thus enabling substantial savings in investments and operating costs due to the shorter routes of pipes and conduits.

The open space between the two rows of halls was also reduced. This resulted in a considerable slimming down of the entrance areas. In this context, the multi-storey car park with its three bridges spanning the motorway was simplified to two »fingers«, enabling significant additional savings.

Legal factors

In the lead-up to execution, there were numerous pockets of resistance as well as conflicts against a background of expropriation which the farmers were being threatened with. There was also the encroachment on the planning sovereignty of the local communities concerned. The public discussions, the unexpected opposition and the planning approval procedure – the documentation for which filled more than 180 folders – became an acid test for the new planning team which had been quickly cobbled together.

Bis zum Planfeststellungsbeschluss und der Bestätigung von dessen Rechtmäßigkeit wurde die Planung von den ständigen Erörterungen und den gerichtlichen Auseinandersetzungen begleitet. Beim daraufhin erfolgten Startschuss im Jahr 2004 lagen die Ausführungspläne schon weitestgehend in der Schublade. Die dadurch erlangte Sicherheit bei Kosten und Terminen, vor allem aber bei der Planung erbrachte einen veritablen planerischen Vorsprung vor dem Eintreffen der ersten Baumaschinen und machte das Großprojekt damit beherrschbarer.

Realisierung
Spannende Themen der Realisierung waren entwurfsbedingt die Höhenstufen auf dem Baugelände, die Dächer und Konstruktionen der Hallen, die Montage des Parkhauses und die Baulogistik. Die folgenden Geschichten erzählen von Erde, Beton und Stahl, von 250.000 Quadratmetern neuer Messe auf mehr als 50 Hektar Ackerland.

»Baggern bis zum Sonnenuntergang« lautete ein geflügeltes Wort auf der Baustelle, und tatsächlich: Die ersten Wochen und Monate sah man nichts als das Herausschälen der vom Entwurf vorgegebenen Geländeterrassen, das Anheben von Straßen, das Ausschachten von Gruben und das Anlegen von Erdmieten. Hunderte von Lastwagenladungen Erde wurden abtransportiert, säuberlich getrennt nach ihrer Qualität und späterer Wiederverwendung. Der Messeberg »Monte Messelino« war mehrere Jahre Zeichen eines Bauplatzes, der lange eine reine Erdbaustelle war.

In its requirements regarding the extent and depth of the actual planning, the procedure went far beyond the tried and tested practice of the standard building approval process and dealt with all the aspects in one single go. The required bundling of issues relating to traffic, environmental protection, ecology, fire protection, statics, urban planning and so on necessitated the rapid build-up of an effective interdisciplinary team. Even in this early phase, the procedure demanded a geographically precise specification of the trade fair centre with regard to layout, dimensions and proportions which – later hardly changeable – became the basis for all further plans and for the planners as well.

Until the plans were ratified in the planning procedure and their legality was confirmed, planning was accompanied by continual discussions and legal disputes. When the go-ahead was given in 2004, most of the plans for execution were already in the bag. The resulting certainty pertaining to costs, deadlines and, especially, planning enabled a veritable leap forward in planning before the first excavators arrived. This, in turn, made the large-scale project much easier to handle.

Realisation
Among the fascinating aspects of realisation were the different height levels, the hall roofs and their diverse technical features as well as the construction of the multi-storey car park over the motorway and the logistics for the whole project. The following stories tell of earth, concrete and steel, of 250,000 square meters of new trade fair centre on more than 50 hectares of farmland.

»Excavators until the sun goes down«, was an inspired phrase heard on the building site. And this was indeed the case. During the first weeks and months, there was nothing to see except roads being raised, pits being excavated, large mounds of earth being piled up and machines digging out the terraces as required by the design. Hundreds of truckloads of earth were taken away to be sorted according to quality and the later method of re-use. The site of the trade fair centre, jokingly called the »Monte Messelino« (little trade fair mountain), was an earthworks construction site for a very long time rather than an actual »building« site.

01

02

03

04

01–04 Kranarbeiten an Eingangshalle Ost
und Parkhausbrücken

Crane work at the eastern entrance hall and
bridges of the multi-storey car park

Seite 070–071
Spätschicht im Herbst 2005

Page 070–071
Late shift in autumn 2005

Seite 072–073
Montage der Randträger an einer
Standardhalle im Januar 2006

Page 072–073
Mounting of the edge girders on a
standard hall in January 2006

01

02

03

04

Der Anfang der Bauarbeiten erfolgte nicht ohne Grund im Bereich des Congresscenters und der angrenzenden Tiefgarage. Im tiefsten Punkt der gesamten Neuen Messe wurden umfängliche Ausschachtungs- und Gründungsarbeiten notwendig, teilweise sogar nicht unerhebliche Sprengungen im anstehenden Fels. Auch hier wurde für die leicht wirkende oberirdische Erscheinung der Konstruktion viel Vorarbeit im Untergrund notwendig. Beim Congresscenter liegt die Besonderheit zunächst in dem weit auskragenden Dach. Die Sichtbetonflächen der Auflastpunkte im Foyer und der Wände stellten große Anforderungen an die ausführenden Baufirmen. Durch die Unterbringung der gesamten Gebäudetechnik in den Untergeschossen waren für die tief liegenden Bereiche besondere Gründungsaufwendungen mit umfassenden Sprengungen notwendig.

Fast 500.000 Kubikmeter Beton wurden als Unterbau für die Strukturen von Stahl, Glas und Metall benötigt. Für diesen Beton ist eine eigene Architektur geschaffen worden. Ein ganzes Betonwerk versorgte zwei Jahre lang die Baustelle. Die Messe zeigt nur die Leichtigkeit des Stahls; die Schwere des Betons bleibt verborgen, in den Fundamenten, Stützmauern, Bodenplatten und Decken. Man sah sie in der Bauphase in den Jahren 2004 und 2005. Nun gehören sie zu den unsichtbaren Katakomben der Technikwelt. Heute sind nur noch die sichtbaren Stützmauern und Höhenstufen Zeugen der Betonwelt.

It was not without reason that the construction work began in the area of the international congress centre and the adjacent underground car park. At the lowest point of the entire new trade fair centre, extensive excavation and foundation-laying work was necessary and, sometimes, even explosives had to be used to remove the rock substrate encountered. Here as well, a lot of preparatory work was necessary before the apparently light construction work above ground could be started. With regard to the congress centre, the outstanding feature is the projecting roof. The fair-faced concrete surfaces of the walls and the load-bearing sections in the foyer placed difficult demands on the construction companies doing the work. As all the technical building systems and equipment were accommodated in the basements, special foundation-laying work with extensive blasting was necessary for the low lying areas.

Almost 500,000 cubic metres of concrete were needed as substructure for the steel, glass and metal structures above ground. Special architecture was created for this concrete alone and, for two years, an entire concrete factory supplied the needs of the construction site. The trade fair centre only reveals the lightness of steel; the heaviness of the concrete remains well concealed – in the foundations, supporting walls, floor slabs and ceilings. In the construction phase in the years 2004 and 2005, it was still possible to see them. But now, they are hidden in the invisible catacombs housing the technical equipment. Today, the visible supporting walls and terraces are the only reminders of the world of concrete beneath the surface.

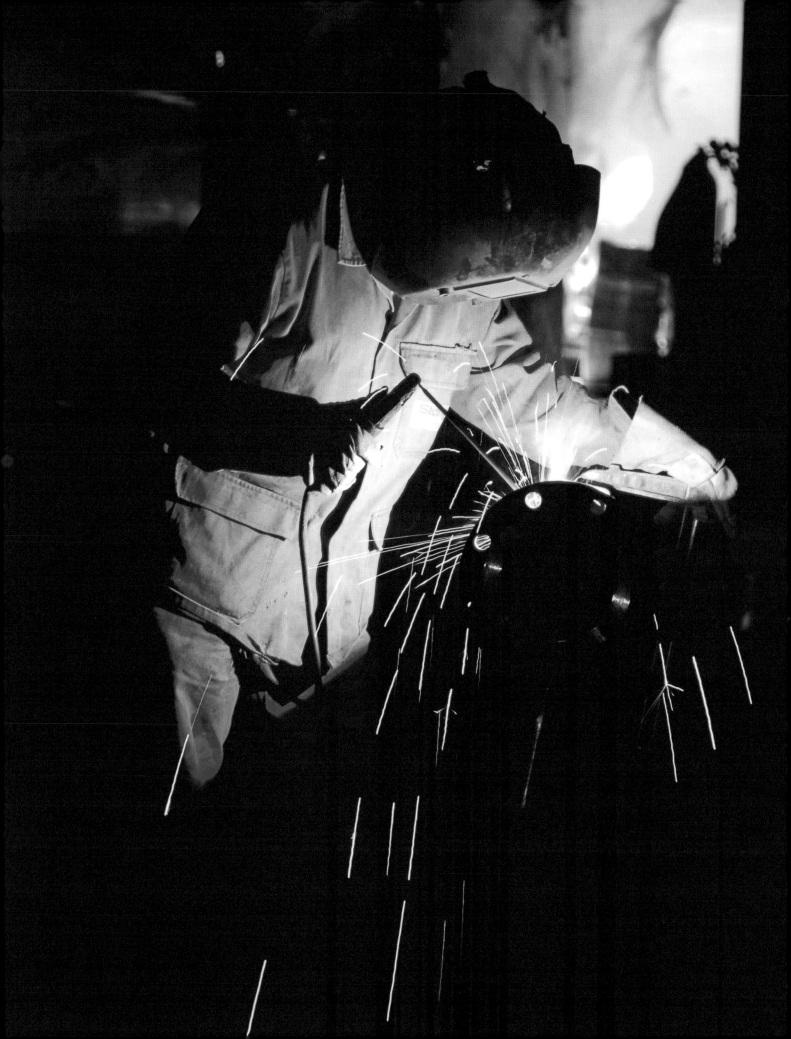

Das bestimmende Gestaltungselement der Messe ist jedoch der Stahl, denn große Aufgaben erfordern große Spannweiten, die besser mit Stahlbau zu meistern sind. Wie bei anderen Großprojekten dominiert die Konstruktion formal und architektonisch das Erscheinungsbild. Der Anstieg des Stahlpreises durch den chinesischen Bauboom war nach fertiggestellter Planung zwar kostentreibend, aber kein Hinderungsgrund. Insgesamt wurden bei dem Projekt 50.000 Tonnen sichtbarer Konstruktionsstahl eingebaut. In einer eigenen Feldwerkstatt wurden vorgefertigte Rohelemente unter Zeltdächern zusammengeschweißt und Portalkräne hievten die bis zu 40 Tonnen schweren Einzelstücke zwischen Tieflader, Zelt und Lagerflächen hin und her.

Der natürliche Pinselschwung der Kalligrafie geht von unten nach oben, von links nach rechts; so entstanden die Messehallen – auf dem Papier. Die schöne Form entsprach dem Gedanken von der Leichtigkeit fliegender Teppiche, die eine offene Messelandschaft bedecken. Dass zugbeanspruchte Strukturen Minimalkonstruktionen sind, ist für jedermann nachvollziehbar. Doch dass der eigentliche Kraftaufwand dabei in den Boden verlagert und dort beherrscht werden muss, macht besondere Aufwendungen erforderlich.

Die Aufnahme der Kräfte wurde bei den Hallen durch die Ausbildung der Technikkanäle als Gründungskörper an den Hallenlängsseiten gelöst, die mithilfe von Erdankern die großen Zugkräfte aufnehmen.

And yet the dominant design element of the trade fair centre is the steel, the reason being that large projects require large span widths and, for this purpose, steel is still the best material there is. As in other large projects, the structural design is what determines the appearance both formally and architecturally. The rise in the price of steel due to the Chinese building boom after the plans had been completed drove up the costs but failed to impair progress. Altogether, 50,000 metric tons of visible construction steel was used for the project. In a special field workshop, prefabricated untreated parts were welded together beneath tent roofs while gantry cranes lifted the individual sections, some of which weighed up to 40 metric tons, back and forth between the low-bed trucks, the tent and the storage areas.

The natural swing of the brush in calligraphy goes from top to bottom, from left to right. This is how the trade fair halls were created – at least on paper. The fascinating form is like the lightness of flying carpets covering the open landscape of the trade fair centre. The fact that structures subjected to tensile stress are minimal constructions can be understood by anyone. But that the actual force exerted is transferred into the ground and has to be absorbed there necessitates a series of special constructional measures.

The problem of force absorption in the case of the halls was solved by designing the equipment conduits as parts of the foundations along the long sides of the halls. With the help of »deadmen«, they are able to absorb the enormous tensile forces that are exerted by the construction.

Seite 076–077
Die Parkhausbrücken wachsen
über die Autobahn

Page 076–077
The bridges of the multi-storey
car park gradually extending over
the motorway

02

01

03

04

01–02 Brückenschlag über die Autobahn
im Herbst 2005

Bridge over the motorway
in autumn 2005

03 Betonieren des Parkhausbodens

Concreting of the floor in the
multi-storey car park

04 Aufbringen des Substrats für die
Dachbegrünung der Standardhallen

Application of the substrate for
the vegetation on the roof of the
standard halls

01

02

04

03

Ungewöhnlich in diesem Zusammenhang ist auch die Bodenplatte, die erst nach Montage der Dachkonstruktionen betoniert wurde. Zu anfällig war das gewählte Herstellungsverfahren der Böden in geglättetem Beton und zu rabiat der Baubetrieb, als dass man die Böden wie sonst üblich gleich zu Anfang hätte gießen können. Sie wurden zusammen mit den Spartenkanälen zur Medienversorgung nach Montage von Fassaden und Dach parallel zu den bereits angelaufenen Ausbauarbeiten hergestellt.

Schwerstarbeit hatten die Kräne in der Hochhalle zu leisten. Deren 168 Meter langer und 9 Meter hoher Hauptträger ist eine Spitzenleistung der Ingenieure und der Stahlbaufirma. Bei der Endmontage des Mittelsegments ereignete sich unglücklicherweise ein Unfall, der einen Monteur das Leben kostete.

Dass die geknickten Hallenfassaden mit ihrem fast automobilen Charakter eher an eine Karosserie erinnern, ist architektonische Absicht. Realisiert wurden die Fassaden auf der Grundlage des Stahlbaus. Bereits im frühen Stadium erfüllte der Stahlbauer mit der Konstruktion aus geknickten Stahlträgern die konstruktiven Voraussetzungen für deren Montage.

Einen weiteren Superlativ erlebte das Projekt beim Bau der Parkhausbrücke, als die beiden Parkhausfinger mit einem Gewicht von mehreren tausend Tonnen bei laufendem Verkehr über die Autobahn A 8 geschoben wurden.

Zeichenhaft für die ökologische Ausrichtung der Architektur wurden die geschwungenen Dächer anschließend begrünt und mit Bäumen bepflanzt – semiotisches und natürliches Zeichen einer von Technik dominierten Konstruktion.

What is also unusual in this context is the floor slab. It was not filled in with concrete until the roof constructions had been mounted. The selected method for making the floors with smoothed concrete was too sensitive and the building work was too rough to allow the concrete floors to be poured in at the beginning as is usually done. Together with the equipment conduits for the supply of diverse media, they were built after the facades and roof had been fitted and at the same time as the finishing work which had already been started.

The crane in the high hall had the heaviest work to do. Its 168 metre long and 9 meter high beam was an outstanding achievement of the engineers and the company responsible for the steel construction work. When the middle segment was being completed, an unfortunate accident occurred causing a fitter to lose his life.

The fact that the bent hall facades which almost look like a car are reminiscent of a chassis was the explicit intention of the architects. The facades were built on the basis of the steel structure. Even at an early stage, the construction of the bent steel beams by the steel builder met all the constructional requirements for their later installation.

Another superlative in the project was the construction of the multi-storey car park bridge. The two »fingers« of the car park weighed several thousand metric tons but were pushed over the A8 motorway without the traffic having to be stopped.

As a sign of the ecological intent of the architecture, the sweepingly curved roofs were then planted with greenery and trees – a semiotic and natural symbol for a construction dominated by its engineering aspects.

**Halb Diplomatie,
halb Sachverstand**
  Thomas Jaißle vom
  Projektsteuerer
  Drees & Sommer im
  Gespräch mit Falk Jaeger

**Half diplomacy,
half expertise**
  Thomas Jaißle from
  project controller,
  Drees & Sommer
  talking to Falk Jaeger

Halb Diplomatie, halb Sachverstand
Thomas Jaißle vom Projektsteuerer Drees & Sommer im Gespräch mit Falk Jaeger

Half diplomacy, half expertise
Thomas Jaißle from project controller, Drees & Sommer talking to Falk Jaeger

FJ Was versteht man unter Projektmanagement?

TJ Projektmanagement ist nichts anderes als die Übernahme von delegierbaren Bauherrenaufgaben durch externe Fachleute, die die Kapazität und das Know-how dazu beisteuern. Die Projektgesellschaft Neue Messe wollte als Bauherr und Auftraggeber möglichst schlank bleiben. Drees & Sommer ist 1999 in der 2. Phase des Architektenwettbewerbs mit den Kostenschätzungen der Wettbewerbsentwürfe beauftragt worden. Ich habe damals die Meinung vertreten, dass es richtig ist, neben architektonischen und funktionalen Kriterien auch die Kostenfrage schon im Wettbewerb nach vorne zu bringen, um möglichst frühzeitig auch in dieser Frage eine Entscheidungsbasis zu schaffen. Der eigentliche Projekteinstieg kam für uns nach einem europaweiten VOF-Verfahren und nach Abschluss des Architektenwettbewerbs, als die drei Entwürfe von den Architekturbüros Hotz, Kaupp und Wulf als Preisträger ausgewählt waren. Wir hatten damals vorgeschlagen, eine Optimierungsphase anzuschließen, aus der sich dann der Bauentwurf ergeben sollte.

FJ Welche Aufgaben hatte Drees & Sommer in dieser Phase? Haben Sie die drei Teams beraten?

TJ Gemeinsam mit dem Bauherrn hatten wir bereits zum Abschluss des Architektenwettbewerbs bei den drei Entwürfen jeweils die Optimierungspotenziale lokalisiert. Beim Entwurf von Wulf haben wir beispielsweise damals schon gesagt: Die Gebäude sind sehr in die Filderlandschaft eingegraben, wenn wir sie etwas anheben, sparen wir Millionen und erreichen gleichzeitig ein besseres Erdmassenmanagement. Wir waren für die Architekten mit unseren Erfahrungen aus vergleichbaren Großprojekten Hilfesteller und Berater.

Darüber hinaus war eine wesentliche Aufgabe, die terminliche Abwicklung des Messeprojekts vorauszudenken, sprich einen Rahmenterminplan mit der Projektgesellschaft Neue Messe zu vereinbaren. Eine weitere Aufgabe war, frühzeitig die vertraglichen Eckdaten mit den drei verbliebenen Wettbewerbern zu verhandeln und die weitere Zusammenstellung des Planerteams über europaweite Ausschreibungen vorzubereiten. Es galt, eine Abwicklungsstrategie aufzubauen, wie das Planerteam aufgestellt werden soll und in welchen für die einzelnen Planer handhabbaren Teilprojekten das Bauvorhaben dann ablaufen sollte. Denn unser Ansatz war, das Riesenprojekt in Teile zu zerlegen, die für den Menschen letztlich wieder begreifbar und beherrschbar sind.

FJ What is project management exactly?

TJ Project management is nothing other than the performance of a client's tasks by external specialists who possess the necessary capacity as well as the relevant know-how. Being both the client and the contract-awarding party, the project company Neue Messe wanted to avoid being caught up in too many details. In 1999, in the 2nd phase of the architectural competition, Drees & Sommer was engaged to carry out an estimate of the costs involved in the designs. It was right to focus on the question of costs, as well as on architectural and functional criteria, early on in the competition in order to create a basis for a decision on this issue as quickly as possible. We actually came into the picture after a Europe-wide invitation to tender for the project and after the architectural competition had been completed when the three designs from the architect's offices Hotz, Kaupp and Wulf had been selected as the winners. We had proposed adding on a phase of optimisation from which the concrete architectural design was then to be derived.

FJ What did Drees & Sommer have to do in this phase? Did they provide the three teams with advice?

TJ At the end of the architectural competition, we and the clients had already pinpointed the potential for improvement exhibited by each of the three designs. In the case of Wulf's design, for example, we said that the buildings to be erected in the Filder landscape were sunk very deep into the ground and that, if we raised them just a little, we would save a great deal of money and also be in a better position to manage the excavated earth. Another important part of our job was to think in advance about how the trade fair project was to be handled chronologically. In other words, we had to agree on a time frame with the project company Neue Messe. The fundamental contractual details also had to be negotiated with the three remaining competitors and preparations for the other parties who were to join the planning team had to be made by means of invitations to tender which were open to bidders from all over Europe. The aim was to develop a strategy for creating the team of planners and dividing the construction project into sub-projects which the individual planners would be able to handle. Our approach was to break down the huge project into parts which people would be able to understand and easily cope with.

FJ   So sind dann Leonhardt, Andrä und Partner noch hinzugekommen?

TJ   Neben diesem Büro sind die Büros Mayr + Ludescher und Boll und Partner als Tragwerksplaner beauftragt worden. Eine Reihe weiterer Fachplaner, die zum Beispiel für die technische Gebäudeausrüstung verantwortlich waren, hatten sich jeweils bei den europaweiten Ausschreibungen durchgesetzt und ergänzten das Planungsteam.

FJ   Geschieht das grundsätzlich im Sinne der »Gewaltenteilung«, dass man die Vergabe der Planungsleistungen nicht dem Architekten überlässt, oder gäbe es auch große Architekturbüros, die das intern leisten könnten?

TJ   Das ist eine Frage der Abwicklungsstrategie. Es hätte vielleicht auch die Möglichkeit gegeben, alles in die Hand eines Generalplaners zu legen. Ich glaube aber, dass die Entscheidung richtig war, die Planungsaufträge einzeln zu vergeben, weil der Bauherr dadurch näher am Planungsgeschehen und an den Entscheidungen dran ist. Wir können bei einem derartigen Planungsprozess Erfahrungswerte aus einer Vielzahl von Großprojekten beisteuern.

FJ   Gab es in dieser Phase Verzögerungen, mit denen Sie nicht gerechnet haben?

TJ   Die gab es in der Tat, denn das ursprüngliche Terminziel des Bauherrn war ja, die Gebäude bis Mitte des Jahres 2005 fertig zu stellen. Aber das zweistufige Planfeststellungsverfahren mit tausenden von Einsprüchen, von denen jeder einzelne beantwortet werden musste, und die Enteignungsverfahren im Zusammenhang mit dem Grunderwerb haben den Fahrplan gründlich durcheinandergebracht. Um diese Zeitspanne sinnvoll zu nutzen, haben wir die Planung parallel weiter vorangetrieben und das erste Ausschreibungspaket auf den Markt gebracht. Allerdings konnte niemand den Baubeginntermin definitiv nennen. Im Grunde genommen war das eine einmalige Geschichte, Kostenziel und Terminziel zu definieren unter den Bedingungen eines komplexen Verfahrens, von dem man nicht wusste, wie es ausgehen würde. Im Straßenbau ist das gang und gäbe, aber nicht bei Hochbauprojekten.

FJ   So this is where Leonhardt, Andrä und Partner came in?

TJ   Apart from them, Mayr + Ludescher and Boll und Partner had been engaged to plan the load-bearing structure. A whole series of other specialist planners who were responsible for the technical building equipment, for example, had been successful in the invitations to tender and supplemented the planning team.

FJ   Is it based on the idea of »power sharing« when the awarding of contracts for planning services is not left up to the architect or are there large architect's office which can do this internally?

TJ   That is a question of handling strategy. It would also have been possible, perhaps, to put everything in the hands of a general planner. I believe that the decision to award planning orders to individual planners was the right one because this means that the client stays closer to the planning activities and decision-making process. In such a planning process, we are able to contribute the experience we have gathered in many large projects of this kind.

FJ   Were there any delays in this phase which you did not expect?

TJ   There were indeed, as the client's original deadline for completion of the building was the middle of 2005, However, the two-stage planning approval procedure with its thousands of objections – each of which had to be answered individually – combined with the procedure involved in the compulsory purchase of land messed up the timetable considerably. In order to make best use of the time available, we continued to push ahead with planning at the same time and brought the first bid invitation package onto the market. However, no-one was able to name a definite date for the start of construction. Basically, the situation was unique in that a cost target and deadline had to be defined in the framework of a complex procedure, the outcome of which was unknown. In road construction, this is perfectly normal practice, but not in architectural projects.

FJ Schon in der Planung begann Ihre Arbeit als Termin- und Kostenkontrolleur?

TJ Das würde ich nicht nur als Kontrolle bezeichnen. Wir haben unsere Aufgaben immer so verstanden, dass man gemeinsam mit dem Bauherrn Ziele vorgibt und dem Planungsteam bei der Umsetzung dieser Ziele mit unter die Arme greift. Also nicht in der Funktion eines Kontrolleurs, sondern eines Beraters, der aber natürlich die Aufgabe hat, die Ziele nicht aus dem Auge zu verlieren. Wir haben, glaube ich, eine Art der effektiven Zusammenarbeit gefunden, zum Beispiel mit den regelmäßigen Besprechungsrunden, bei denen alle Probleme zur Sprache kommen. Das magische Dreieck Kosten – Termine – Qualitäten lässt sich nicht auseinandernehmen. In kritischen Situationen haben wir es auch geschafft, den Routineablauf zu durchbrechen, und gesagt, lass uns mal ganz bewusst rausgehen, nach Haigerloch etwa, und in einem Workshop nur ein spezielles Thema begutachten. Also raus in eine andere Arbeitsumgebung, in der man den Kopf etwas freier hat und Dinge anders sehen und angehen kann. Das Team bei der Stange zu halten, immer wieder in Optimierungsrunden gemeinsam reinzugehen, die SMK als Nutzer einzubinden, das war ein Prozess, der sich über all die Jahre hingezogen hat.

FJ Wie hat die Politik eigentlich akzeptiert, dass das Projekt dann doch so teuer werden wird?

TJ Gut, wir haben Vergleichsdaten von anderen Messen wie Leipzig und München herangezogen, die auch den Anspruch haben, auf dem internationalen Messeparkett mitspielen zu wollen. Letztlich war das die einzige Möglichkeit, die Entscheidungsgremien über das Benchmarking auf der einen Seite und über Kostenoptimierung auf der anderen Seite davon zu überzeugen, dass der ursprüngliche Kostenrahmen zu eng war. Das Bauprogramm umfasste ja neben den eigentlichen Standardmessehallen auch das Congresscenter, dieses riesige Parkhaus über der A 8 und die komplette verkehrliche Infrastruktur. Für eine Milliarde DM, so haben wir argumentiert, ist die geplante Kernmesse durchaus darstellbar, allerdings ohne die umgebende Infrastruktur, wie zum Beispiel das Parkhaus, die neuen Straßen, Tunnel und Brücken. Aber es hat viel, viel Überzeugungsarbeit gebraucht und das war ein Schwerpunkt unserer Arbeit. So etwas geht weit über das reine technische Fachwissen hinaus. Ich denke, 50 Prozent unseres Jobs sind Kommunikation, Psychologie und Diplomatie und die restlichen 50 Prozent sind planerischer und technischer Sachverstand.

FJ Your work as time-schedule and cost controller started as early as the planning phase?

TJ I would not call it control. We always understood our job to be specifying goals together with the client and helping the planning team to implement these goals. In other words, we did not act as a controller but as a consultant, who nevertheless had the task of keeping an eye on the goals. I believe we found a way of working effectively together, for example with the regular meetings in which any problems were discussed. The magic triangle of costs, deadlines and quality cannot be split up. In critical situations, we also managed to break with routine and said let's go out for a change, to Haigerloch for example, and think about only one special topic in a workshop. The idea was to find a new working environment where there was less mental pressure, where it was possible to see things differently and explore new approaches. Keeping the team on their toes, taking part in repeated improvement meetings together, involving SMK as the user – that was a process that dragged on over the years.

FJ How did the political establishment eventually accept that the project would be so expensive?

TJ Well, we used data from other trade fairs in places such as Leipzig and Munich which also wanted to be players in the international trade fair scene. In the end, this was the only way of convincing the decision-makers that the original budget was too tight. We also used bench-marking and cost optimization as arguments. The original program for the actual standard trade fair halls had been added to with the congress centre and the huge multi-storey car park over the A8 as well as all the transport infrastructure. For the DM one billion, we argued, the core trade fair which had been planned was feasible but without the surrounding infrastructure, such as the multi-storey car park, the new roads, the tunnels and the bridges. However, it took a lot of persuasion. This was a focal point of our work and requires much more than just specialist technical knowledge. I think that 50% of our job is communication, psychology and diplomacy while the remaining 50% is expertise in planning and technical matters.

FJ   Wie sind Sie mit den Verzögerungen im Planungsablauf umgegangen?

TJ   Den zeitlichen Ablauf des Planfeststellungsverfahrens konnten wir nicht beeinflussen. Unsere Aufgabe war, das Planungsteam vom Frühjahr 2002 bis zum endgültigen Grunderwerb im August 2004 zusammenzuhalten und die Planung weiter zu qualifizieren. Eine schwierige Phase, denn während der langen Zeiträume bestand immer die Gefahr, dass Änderungen hereingetragen werden und es Projektstörungen von außen geben könnte, die es dann aufzufangen gilt. Und man durfte dabei die wesentlichen Ziele nicht aus den Augen verlieren: nämlich das Projekt funktional zu optimieren, ohne die Kosten weggleiten zu lassen und terminlich immer Druck auf der Pipeline zu lassen. Sie glauben gar nicht, wie schwierig es ist, ein Team zu motivieren, das gar nicht absehen kann, ob und wann da oben auf den Fildern überhaupt der Grund und Boden erworben werden kann.

Wir selbst haben die Zeit optimal genutzt, um den späteren Bauablauf zu simulieren, und in zweidimensionalen Plänen sehr detailliert überlegt, wie man die Baufelder angehen kann, wie die Baulogistik aussieht, wo die Baustelleneinrichtungsflächen liegen und wie die Baustelle ver- und entsorgt werden kann. Die gründliche Vorplanung der Bauarbeiten ermöglichte auch die spontanen Änderungen im Bauablauf, die aus verschiedenen Gründen notwendig wurden. Das Know-how für die Krisenbewältigung hat sich unser Büro zum Beispiel beim DaimlerChrysler-Projekt am Potsdamer Platz in Berlin aneignen können.

FJ   Sie haben dann den laufenden Baufortgang und die Baukosten beobachtet?

TJ   Tatsächlich war das ein knallhartes Termin- und Kostencontrolling. Zum Beispiel mussten mehr Flächen als ursprünglich geplant erworben werden. Dies führte zu Mehrkosten beim Grunderwerb. Weil die Kostenobergrenze von 806 Millionen Euro trotz unerwartet hoher Kosten für den Grunderwerb gehalten werden sollte, musste das ganze Team die Mehrkosten durch Optimierungs- und Einsparungsanstrengungen bis zum Ende der Baumaßnahmen auffangen. Wir haben 70 Millionen Euro an Einsparungen realisiert, ohne dass am Raumprogramm, an der Funktionalität oder an der architektonischen Qualität wesentlich gekürzt worden wäre. Der Anspruch an die Architektur wurde von allen hochgehalten und es war ein erklärtes Ziel von Drees & Sommer, an der Architektur nichts kaputt zu sparen. Doch auch bei den Architekten, das muss ich sagen, war die Bereitschaft groß, auf Anregungen und Optimierungsvorschläge einzugehen.

FJ   How did you deal with the delays in planning?

TJ   We were unable to influence the effect of the planning approval procedure on the time needed for planning. It was our task to keep the planning team together from spring 2002 until final purchase of the land in August 2004 and to carry out further planning adjustments. A difficult phase given that changes occurred and external problems which had to be solved also affected the project. At the same time, an eye had to be kept on the central objective, namely to optimise the project in functional terms without allowing the costs to get out of control. You would not believe how difficult it was to motivate a team that did not know if and when land in the Filder area would be purchased.

We used the time to simulate the later construction process and, with the help of two-dimensional diagrams, gave detailed consideration to how the construction sites were to be handled, what the construction logistics would be, where the areas for the construction site equipment were to be placed and how construction site services were to be provided. This thorough advance planning also enabled spontaneous changes to the construction process, which became necessary for various reasons. We had gained this know-how for handling crises from the DaimlerChrysler project in Potsdamer Platz in Berlin, for example.

FJ   Did you monitor the ongoing construction process and the construction costs?

TJ   This was a matter of pure cost controlling. For example, more land had to be acquired than had originally been planned. This led to additional costs for the purchase of land. Because the upper cost limit of 806 million euros had to be kept to in spite of unexpectedly higher costs for the land, the whole team had to struggle to absorb the additional costs by making savings right up to the end of construction. We achieved savings of 70 million euros without have to make any significant cut-backs in respect of the space used, functionality or architectural quality. Everyone wanted to maintain the high architectural quality and it was one of the declared goals of Drees & Sommer to avoid making savings that would diminish it in any way. But I also have to say that the architects were very open to new ideas and suggestions for improvement.

Sanfte Führung,
unmerkliche Hierarchien
Ein Rundgang durch
die Architektur der Messe

Gentle guidance and
imperceptible hierarchies
A tour through the
architecture of
the trade fair centre

Sanfte Führung, unmerkliche Hierarchien
Ein Rundgang durch die Architektur der Messe

Gentle guidance and imperceptible hierarchies
A tour through the architecture of the trade fair centre

Ob beim ersten Blick aus dem Auto auf dem Zubringer von Stuttgart, auf der Autobahn von Karlsruhe oder von München/Ulm her oder gar aus dem Flugzeug im Anflug auf Echterdingen, die Messe fällt ins Auge und fesselt mit ihren ungewohnten Bauformen den Blick. Das Bild einer Landschaft beschwingter Dächer prägt sich ein, die den Ort charakterisieren und ihn unverwechselbar machen. Hinzu kommt das eindrucksvolle Parkhaus, das mit zwei riesigen Fingern über die Autobahn greift und mit seiner nie gesehenen Form und mit dem signifikanten monumentalen Schriftzug »BOSCH« für alle Autofahrer, die auf der A 8 unterwegs sind, längst zur Landmarke geworden ist.

Dabei sind es nicht spektakuläre, auf Schau getrimmte und auf Sensationseffekte spekulierende Bauwerke, die sich hier tief ins optische Gedächtnis einsenken, es sind Bauformen, die ganz unangestrengt aus der Aufgabe und ihrer konstruktiven Lösung heraus gebildet wurden. Formen, die ihrerseits den Ort, die Umgebung, eine ganze Landschaft prägen und wiederum in ihr gebunden sind.

Zwei Spuren in der Landschaft der Filderebene, zwei Reihen von Messehallen, verlängert über die Autobahn durch die beiden Finger des Parkhauses in Richtung eines Blickpunkts am östlichen Horizont. Zweier Blickpunkte eigentlich, denn die Spuren liegen nicht parallel, wie sie jeder Architekt spontan aufs Papier skizziert hätte und wie schon hundert Messeanlagen gebaut wurden, sie streben auseinander, öffnen sich der Landschaft oder besser noch ziehen den Landschaftsraum ins Messeleben herein.

Das neue Stuttgarter Ausstellungsgelände hat eine Besonderheit gegenüber allen anderen deutschen Messen: 20 Meter Höhendifferenz, die die Architekten nicht als Hindernis, sondern als Chance gesehen haben. Während die Konkurrenten im Wettbewerb die schiefe Ebene zu überspielen versuchten, nahmen Wulf & Partner die Herausforderung an, bauten sie funktional in ihr Konzept ein und nutzten sie, um der Messe den Landschaftsbezug zu geben, den alle anderen Messen vermissen lassen. Zudem geben die Abstufungen dem Auge Hilfen zur maßstäblichen Gliederung der Anlage, auch dies ein Vorteil gegenüber den ungeteilten, seriell endlos scheinenden Anlagen anderer Messen.

Whether you are travelling on the access road from Stuttgart by car, arriving on the motorway from Karlsruhe or Munich, or even if you are looking out of a plane on the descent to Stuttgart airport, the unusual form of the trade fair centre immediately catches the eye and captures your attention. The built landscape composed of wide, sweeping roofs imposes its personality on the location and, at the same time, makes it unforgettable. The overall picture is enhanced by the highly impressive multi-storey car park whose two enormous »fingers« stretch out and reach over the motorway. With its unprecedented shape and monumental »BOSCH« sign, it has long since become a landmark for all drivers on the A8.

The buildings are not spectacular, made for show or intentionally sensational nor were they specifically designed to engrave themselves deep in the memory. They are structures whose form results – in a completely unforced manner – from the functions they perform and from their underlying engineering design. They lend character to the location, the surroundings and the immediately adjacent landscape and, in turn, they are embedded and intimately incorporated in them.

One viewpoint is of two tracks imprinted on the landscape of the Filder plain, with two rows of trade fair halls and extensions over the motorway in the form of the two »fingers« of the multi-storey car park pointing in the direction of the eastern horizon. But, in fact, there are two viewpoints in that the tracks are not parallel to each other. Any architect would have spontaneously sketched them in a parallel arrangement and this is how halls are to to be found in hundreds of trade fair centres all over the world. In this case, however, they distinctly diverge from each other, opening themselves up to the landscape or, better still, pulling the countryside itself into the interior life of the trade fair.

The new Stuttgart exhibition centre has something special about it compared to all other German trade fair facilities, namely a 20 metre height difference. The architects saw this not as a hindrance but as an opportunity to be exploited. Whereas the competitors in the competition tried to gloss over the incline, Wulf & Partner accepted the challenge, incorporated it functionally in their design and used it to relate the trade fair centre and the

Seite 086
LKW-Zufahrten in die Hallen sind
signalrot markiert

Page 086
The access roads that are intended
for trucks and heavy-goods
vehicles and lead into the halls are
marked with a bright red colour

Messe der kurzen Wege

Taxifahrer werden von der Stuttgarter Messe nicht in gewohntem Maß profitieren. Vom Flugsteig mit dem Trolley zum Congresscenter? Kein Problem und ein kürzerer Weg als in Frankfurt der vom Jet zum Taxi. Vom ICE zum Messeeingang (wenn die Strecke in einigen Jahren fertiggestellt sein wird)? Schneller als das Umsteigen im Berliner Hauptbahnhof vom ICE zur S-Bahn. Von der Autobahn zum Messestand? Kommt nur darauf an, wie flott die Parkhausschranke arbeitet. Die kurzen und schnellen Wege sind einer der gewichtigsten Pluspunkte der neuen schwäbischen Landesmesse.

Dreh- und Angelpunkt ist dabei der Vorplatz, die Messepiazza, als Entree in die Welt der Messe. Alle Besucher kommen hier zusammen, jene vom Flughafen und von der S-Bahn durch die Unterführung der Flughafenstraße, jene vom künftigen ICE-Bahnhof, jene aus dem Parkhaus und jene aus der Tiefgarage unter dem Platz. Die Piazza ist konvex gewölbt, »wie ein Ausschnitt der Erdkugel«, sagen die Architekten, das weitet den Blick. Sie heißt willkommen mit all den Attributen des Messebetriebs, mit Fahnen und Hinweisstelen, aber auch mit den temporären Elementen eines Marktbetriebs, mit denen jede einzelne Veranstaltung auf sich aufmerksam macht. In Planung, aber noch nicht realisiert ist das gläserne Vordach. Wie ein fliegender Teppich soll das gewellte Vordach auf neun schlanken Masten über der Ecke des Eingangsgebäudes schweben, mehr ein Zeichen, eine Metapher als ein Schutzdach, mehr zeigend als bergend. Es ist als Empfangsgeste des Foyers gedacht, das sich ansonsten einer vordergründigen Torsymbolik enthält.

Die Ziele stehen dem Ankömmling auf der Messepiazza alle vor Augen, das Congresscenter mit seiner dominanten Panoramafront, der Haupteingang mit seiner Empfangshalle, das Parkhaus, das auch die Fluggäste benutzen, und das Verwaltungsgebäude der Messe zur Rechten, es gibt keine Irritationen, keine Orientierungsschwierigkeiten, keine Umwege. Hinweisschilder sind eigentlich nicht notwendig, die Architektur spricht für sich.

landscape to each other, an achievement apparent at no other trade fair centre. Moreover, the terraced gradations help the eye to give the site a sense of scale. This is another advantage over the uninterrupted, seemingly endless layouts of other trade fair venues.

Short distances

Taxi drivers will not be able to profit from the Stuttgart trade fair centre in their usual manner. From the airport gate with a trolley to the congress centre? No problem. And the distance is shorter than from jet to taxi in Frankfurt airport. From the ICE to the entrance of the trade fair centre (when the track is completed in several years)? Faster than changing from the ICE to the municipal transit system in Berlin's central railway station. From the motorway to the trade fair stand? This only depends on how fast the car park barrier works. The short and quickly completed distances are one of the most important benefits of the new Swabian state trade fair centre.

The place where everything comes together is the forecourt, the piazza which serves as the main entrance to the entire trade fair centre. This is where all the visitors will come together – from the airport, from the rapid transit system under the airport access road, from the future ICE railway station, as well as from the multi-storey car park and the underground car park directly beneath the square. The piazza has a convex shape like »part of a globe«, say the architects; it helps to widen the view. It welcomes arriving guests with all the attributes of a trade fair venue – with flags and information columns and with the temporary elements of a market operation, used by each individual event to draw attention to itself. The glass canopy is being planned but has not yet been made. Like a flying carpet, the wave-shaped canopy resting on nine masts hovers over the corner of the entrance building, more of a symbol or metaphor than protective roof, more symbolic than sheltering. It is intended to be the welcoming gesture of the foyer and also represents the idea of a gateway to what lies beyond.

Messepiazza mit Congresscenter links,
Haupteingang und Parkhaus rechts

Trade fair piazza with congress centre on
the left and main entrance and multi-storey
car park on the right

Gute Übersicht in der Eingangshalle erleichtert
die erste Orientierung im Messegelände

The clear layout of the entrance hall facilitates
initial orientation in the trade fair centre

Restaurants im Hanggeschoss verbinden
die Hallen quer zur grünen Achse

Restaurants located on the sloping terrain link
the halls right across the green axis strip

Schon hier wird der Charakter der Architektursprache offenbar. Transparent, trotz der enormen Volumina und Spannweiten mit maximaler Leichtigkeit und ohne jedes Pathos erfüllt die Architektur zurückhaltend und unaufgeregt ihre dienende Funktion.

Die Eingangshalle, ein freier, hoher, durch Oberlichtkuppeln zusätzlich erhellter Raum mit papierdünnem Dach und bleistiftschlanken Stützen, verschafft Überblick. Links der Blick zum Congresscenter, rechts zur Hochhalle, geradeaus breite Treppen hinab zum Basement des Foyers mit dem Blick in den Innenhof, dahinter staffeln sich beiderseits die Standardhallen den Hang hinauf. Über Kopf eine Empore mit Serviceräumen, die Treppen dazu stehen wie elegante Skulpturen zu beiden Seiten parat. Auch hier treten keine Orientierungsprobleme auf, die Besucher können sich der sanften, intuitiven Führung anvertrauen. Natürlich können vorinformierte Besucher gleich den Hinweisen auf die Hallennummern folgen, die sind allgegenwärtig und unmissverständlich gestaltet.

Wege und Hallen

Es gibt eine unmerklich wirksame Hierarchie der Materialien, von kühlen Sichtbetonstützen und -wänden und kraftvollem Stahlgefüge der großen Strukturen und weiten Räume bis zu den warmen Eichenholzfenstern und -türen der kleinen Räume und Rückzugsmöglichkeiten. Auch der in der Halle schwebende Servicebereich ist wie ein Möbel als Box aus Holzrippen mit Fassade aus Glas und Metallpaneelen ausgeführt.

In die Basementebene der Foyerhalle strahlt aus voller Höhe der Glaswand zum Hof das Westlicht. Wasserkaskaden und Begrünung sowie Sitzgelegenheiten und Freitreppen im Hof am Ostende der zentralen Grünachse laden zum Verweilen ein und drohen vom Messebesuch abzulenken. Der eilige Messebesucher begibt sich jedoch nicht geradeaus hinab in das Basement, sondern entscheidet sich für den Weg zu den Ausstellungen – rechts vorbei zu den ungerade, links entlang zu den gerade bezifferten Hallen.

The destinations are clear to see for anyone arriving at the piazza – the congress centre with its dominant panorama facade, the main entrance with its reception hall, the multi-storey car park which air passengers also use, and the administration building on the right. There are no irritations, no difficulties of orientation and no complicated detours. Signs are not actually necessary as the architecture speaks for itself.

This is where the character of the architectural language becomes clear. Transparent, in spite of the enormous sizes and span widths; maximum lightness but without pathos. The architecture performs its predestined function but does so modestly and without show.

The entrance hall is a high open space with skylight cupolas for extra light, a paper-thin roof and pencil-like slim supports, allowing a clear view all round. To the left, there is the congress centre and, to the right, the high hall. Straight ahead, there is a wide staircase leading down into the foyer basement with its view of the inner courtyard. Behind this, there are the standard halls on both sides, resting on the terraces further up the incline. Above the heads of visitors in the foyer, there is a gallery with service rooms with stairs like elegant sculptures leading up to it on both sides. Here as well, there are no problems of orientation and visitors can place their trust in the gentle, intuitive navigation aids provided. Pre-informed visitors can, of course, follow the signs to the hall numbers. They are everywhere and very easy to understand.

Directions and halls

There is an imperceptible hierarchy of materials: from the cool concrete supports and walls and the powerful steel pattern of the large structures and wide-open spaces to the warm oak windows and doors of the small rooms and the places where people can find refuge from the crowds. The service area hovering in the hall is like a piece of furniture in the form of a box with wooden ribs and a facade made of glass and metal panels.

An die Optik der Hallen muss man sich erst gewöhnen. Sie haben einen zeltartigen Charakter, denn die Dächer hängen wie Teppiche über den Teppichstangen – und scheinen ebenso dünn zu sein. Die Hängewerke benötigen kaum Konstruktionshöhe, keine Träger und keine Unterzüge. Nur dünne Zugbänder und eine feine Unterspannung, die der bautechnische Laie glatt übersieht. Von außen, aus gewisser Entfernung, ergibt sich das Bild einer Zeltstadt.

Kritische Blicke werfen nur die Mitarbeiter der Flugsicherung zur Messe herüber. Die großen, gewölbten Dachflächen könnten die Radargeräte irritieren. So haben sich die Architekten entschlossen, die Dächer zum Teil zu begrünen. 100 Kilogramm mit einer Samenmischung dotiertes Erdsubstrat pro Quadratmeter wurden mittels Gebläse aufgebracht. Die grüne Dachhaut sprießt nun in allen Schattierungen, speichert Wasser und unterstützt Wärmedämmung und Kühlung. Weitere Flächen sind von der Messe zur Nutzung mit Solarkollektoren verpachtet.

Im Inneren werden die großen Kräfte deutlich, die zu Boden gebracht werden müssen. Eindrucksvolle haushohe Böcke aus dicken Stahlrohren stemmen die horizontalen Fachwerk-Randträger in die Höhe, an denen die Zugglieder der Dachkonstruktion aufgehängt sind. Eine gerippte Dachhaut hängt über dem Hallenraum und assoziiert die Geborgenheit eines Zeltinneren. Nur die dünnen Seilverspannungen, die Leuchten und Lautsprecher hängen unter der Decke, die hier einmal ihrem Namen gerecht wird, weil sie eben wie eine Decke durchhängt. Ansonsten ist sie frei von Installationen, insbesondere von ebenso voluminösen wie hässlichen Lüftungseinrichtungen – üblicherweise wenig vorteilhafter Deckenschmuck solch weiter Hallen.

Die Lüftung ist unauffällig und gut aufgeräumt in den Längswänden der Halle untergebracht, deren Gliederung die ordnende Hand des Architekten verrät. Alle störenden Details und Gerätschaften sind verhehlt oder wenigstens in gutes Design gekleidet, nichts, auch nicht das kleinste Warnschild wurde dem Zufall überlassen.

In the basement of the foyer, the west light radiates out of the full height of the glass wall to illuminate the courtyard. Water cascades and green areas as well as seats and open staircases in the courtyard at the east end of the central green axis are an invitation to spend time there and threaten to distract people from their actual purpose in coming to the trade fair centre. However, a visitor in a hurry does not go straight down to the basement but decides on which route to take to the exhibitions – to the right to get to the halls with odd numbers, to the left to the ones with even numbers.

The optical impression of the halls takes some getting used to. They have a tent-like character with the roofs suspended like carpets on rods and they appear to be just as thin as well. The suspended elements hardly require height, need no supports and no joists. Only thin tie rods and a delicate underlay which the layman hardly notices. From the outside, the picture at a distance is of a city of tents.

Only the people from the nearby airport's flight control building look critically over to the trade fair centre. The large, curved roof surfaces could irritate the radar instruments. The architects therefore decided to landscape parts of the roofs. 100 kilograms of soil per square meter, planted with a mixture of seeds, was applied with a blower. The green skin of the roofs grows in all shades of colour. Besides absorbing water, it supports heat insulation and cooling. Other surfaces have been rented out by the trade fair centre for use with solar collectors.

On the inside, the enormous forces to be absorbed in the ground become apparent. Impressive, house-high trestles made of thick steel tubes support the horizontal beams at the edges from which the tie rods of the roof construction are suspended. The thin ribbed roof hangs over the hall and evokes associations with the inside of a tent. Only the slim tensioning cables, the lights and loudspeakers are suspended under the sagging ceiling. Otherwise, there are no installations, particularly those bulky ugly ventilation devices that usually decorate such halls.

Schlichte Fluchttreppen und Abluftschächte
werden zu architektonischen Elementen

Simple emergency-exit stairs and air evacuation
ducts become architectural elements

Zwischen den Standardhallen Platz
für Erschließungsstraßen

Space for access roads between
the standard halls

Wie eine leichte Zeltbahn hängt das
Dach über seinen Randträgern

The roof is suspended above its
load-bearing elements at the side like
a lightweight tent canopy

Halle **7**
Hall

Halle 9 → Halle 5
Hall → ↑ ← Hall

Über Treppen und Wandelgänge an der Stirnseite oder direkt an der Längswand führen Wege zur nächsten Halle

Pathways lead to the next hall via staircases and corridors at the front or directly along the longitudinal wall

Manche Fachleute fordern kompromisslos Dunkelhallen und argumentieren, jeder Aussteller würde sein eigenes Licht maßgeschneidert mitbringen und durch natürliches Licht nur gestört werden. Schon aus ökologischen, aber auch aus arbeitspsychologischen Gründen ist es jedoch geboten, die Hallen zumindest in den weitaus überwiegenden Zeitabschnitten ohne unmittelbaren Messebetrieb natürlich zu belichten. Dazu stehen die verglasten Stirnwände und die Obergaden der Längswände zur Verfügung, wobei die dem Sonnenlicht direkt ausgesetzten Gläser zum Schutz vor zu intensiver Einstrahlung mit Pixels bedruckt sind. Bei Bedarf können die Hallen durch Verdunklungseinrichtungen fast vollständig vom Tageslicht abgeschottet werden.

Schichten und Scheiben

Auf den Betonböden mit einer Tragfähigkeit von fünf Tonnen pro Quadratmeter ist jeglicher Schwerlast- und Kranverkehr kein Problem. Alle 6,5 Meter liegt einer der Medienkanäle zur Versorgung der Messestände mit Energie und Kommunikation, die sich in allen Hallen auf eine Gesamtlänge von mehr als 11 Kilometern summieren.

Untereinander verbunden sind die Hallen durch die Galeriegänge beiderseits der zentralen Grünachse des Messegeländes, in deren Verlauf zwei Treppenanlagen die Niveausprünge des Geländes überwinden. Die Gänge haben gläserne Wände gegen die Grünachse und abgehängte Decken, die das für die Architekten typische Prinzip der gestaffelten Schichten und Scheiben variiert. Auch hier wurde nicht zum erstbesten Material gegriffen, sondern die Material- und Farbpalette verrät eine sorgfältige, dennoch ökonomisch orientierte Auswahl.

Durch die Abschüssigkeit des Grundstücks stehen die Hallen auf drei unterschiedlichen Niveaus, was an den Geländesprüngen bergseitig Gelegenheit zu Lagerräumen gibt, die als nahe Pufferflächen zwischen zwei Ausstellungen hochwillkommen sind. Zudem nutzten die Architekten die Möglichkeit, die Hallenanlage an dieser Stelle durch Anlieferstraßen ohne teuere Tunnel zu queren, was viele Umwege durch Umfahren des gesamten Messegeländes erspart. Schließlich wurden die beiden Niveausprünge genutzt, um in der Querspange zwischen den Hallenreihen gedeckte Querverbindungen und Restaurants mit Ausblick ins Grüne anzuordnen, die im Sommer Gartenbetrieb anbieten können. Hohe, schräg stehende Lichtkuppeln wie bei Le Corbusier lugen oben aus dem Dachgarten, versorgen die Restaurants mit zusätzlichem Zenitlicht und helfen, den Kellercharakter zu vermeiden.

The ventilation system is inconspicuously and neatly housed in the hall's long walls, whose structure reveals the orderly hand of the architect. All disturbing details and equipment are concealed or at least clad in a good design. Nothing, not even the smallest warning sign, was left to chance.

Many experts demand uncompromisingly dark halls and argue that exhibitors would bring their own special lighting and would only be disturbed by natural light. For ecological and psychological reasons alone, however, it is better to have halls illuminated with natural light, at least when no exhibitions are taking place, which means most of the time. This is what the front glass walls and upper windows in the longitudinal walls are for, whereby the windows directly exposed to sunlight are printed with pixels as protection against the sun. If necessary, the daylight can be shut out almost completely with the help of window blinds.

Layers and sections

On the concrete floors, which have a load-bearing capacity of five metric tons per square meter, heavy loads and cranes can be moved about without problem. Every 6.5 metres, there is one of the conduits for supplying the trade fair stands with energy and communication lines. Added together, the conduits cover a distance of over 11 kilometres.

The halls are connected to each other by gallery corridors on both sides of the central green axis of the trade fair site, in the course of which two staircases overcome the level differences of the terrain. The corridors have glass walls facing the green axis and are covered by suspended ceilings which vary the typical architects' principle of staggered layers and sections. Here as well, the materials chosen were not the first ones that came to hand; the range of materials and colours betrays a careful yet economical selection.

Due to the inclination of the site, the halls are on three different levels. This enables storage space to be created on the sloping side where the terrain is terraced. This is highly welcome as an intermediate storage area between trade fairs and is also very close to the exhibition

Grüne Messe und große Halle

Besonders bei schönem Wetter bietet der Messepark, die grüne Achse zwischen den beiden Hallenreihen, Gelegenheit für kleine Pausen und zum Abschalten vom Messetrubel. Von den Galeriegängen und von den Querverbindungen aus ist der Park überall zugänglich. Ein Parkweg führt hinab bis zu den Wassertreppen des tiefen Hofs am Osteingang.

Am oberen, westlichen Ende endet der Park an einer kleinen Eingangshalle, dem Westeingang, der separate Zugänge zu Teilmessen in einzelnen Hallen ermöglicht. Ähnlich wie gen Osten hat man hier an der Westvorfahrt den Eindruck einer freien Landschaft, denn die nahen Ränder der benachbarten Ortsteile verschwinden hinter Bäumen und Hügeln. Die Hallen sind von hier aus im Rückblick nach Osten durch voluminöse Luftkanaltürme aus Edelstahl akzentuiert, die wie noble Designobjekte vor den Fassaden positioniert sind.

Wer nicht zur Messe, sondern zum Konzert von Herbert Grönemeyer oder Tokio Hotel, zum WM-Kampf von Wladimir Klitschko oder zu »Wetten dass?« möchte, der wendet sich in der Eingangshalle nach rechts. Die Halle 1, intern auch »Hochhalle« genannt, bietet nicht nur mindestens 14 Meter lichte Höhe für Ausstellungsinstallationen. Sie wird auch als Ort für Publikumsveranstaltungen mit bis zu 17.000 Besuchern genutzt. Die Halle ist bis auf die Lichtraupe über dem Hauptträger in Hallenmitte verdunkelbar.

Der Zugang kann über das Kassen- und Sperrensystem der Messe erfolgen. Nach der Veranstaltung können die Besucher die Halle zügig verlassen, da die Tore an der Ostseite direkt zum Vorplatz hin geöffnet werden können. Auch diese Veranstaltungen mit konzentriertem Zustrom und vor allem gleichzeitigem Abgang vieler Tausend von Besuchern profitiert von der günstigen Lage des Parkhauses und der leistungsfähigen Nahverkehrsverbindung S-Bahn.

Die Großform der Halle 1 lässt unschwer erkennen, dass es sich um zwei gegeneinander gestellte Hängedächer der Standardhallen handelt, deren Mittelwand durch den gewaltigen Hauptträger ersetzt ist. Auch diese Halle kann es an Eleganz und Schönheit mit gleich großen Hallen anderenorts spielend aufnehmen.

area itself. The architects also used the opportunity to insert delivery roads across the hall area without the need for expensive supplementary tunnels. This saves vehicles from having to go on long detours all around the entire trade fair site. Finally, the two level changes were used to place covered cross-connections and restaurants between the long rows of halls. The restaurants provide a view of the surrounding landscape and can offer a beer garden in summer. High, slanting light cupolas like those used by Le Corbusier project out of the roof garden, supplying the restaurants with additional zenith light and helping to prevent a cellar atmosphere from being created.

Green trade fair centre and large hall

Especially during good weather, the park of the trade fair centre, namely the green axis between the two rows of halls, provides an opportunity for short breaks to allow people to switch off from the hullabaloo of the trade fair. The park is accessible from everywhere, from the gallery corridors and the cross-connections. The pathway in the park leads down to the water cascades of the lower courtyard at the east entrance.

At the upper west end, the park comes to an end at a small foyer, the west entrance, which allows separate access to the parts of trade fairs in the individual halls. Like towards the east, the west entrance provides a view of an open, uncluttered landscape as the outskirts of neighbouring municipal districts are hidden behind trees and hills. Looking back from here towards the east, the halls are accentuated by large air-duct towers made of stainless steel which are positioned like exquisite design objects in front of the facades.

Anyone who does not want to go to the trade fair but to a rock concert, to a world-championship boxing match or a televised show has to turn to the right on entering the entrance hall. Hall 1, internally called the »high hall«, has a clear height of 14 metres for exhibition installations. It is used for public events with audiences of up to 17,000 people. Except for the bead of light above the main beam in the middle, the hall can be completely darkened.

Die Wasserkaskade ist Attraktion
und sommerliche Abkühlung im Messepark

The water cascade is a refreshing attraction
in the trade fair park during the Summer

Die Hochhalle
von Süden

The high hall from
the south

Die gläsernen Giebel zeichnen auch bei
Nacht das Bild von den schwingenden Dächern

The glass gables reveal the outlines of the
curved roofs even at night

Konferieren und feiern im Congresscenter

Wer allerdings zum Reden und Konferieren oder zum Feiern großer Feste auf das Messegelände gekommen ist, der kann die Eingangshalle der Messe meiden und das Congresscenter direkt aufsuchen. Die Glasfront unter dem kühn auskragenden, filigranen Dach stellt wie ein Schaufenster den Kongressbetrieb zur Schau. Auf breiter Front öffnen sich die Eingänge zur hellen, großzügigen Foyerhalle. Der Weg führt durch das quer gelagerte Foyer in den Kongresssaal zur Linken oder in die Halle zur Rechten. Der Saal mit seiner edleren Ausstattung mit schwarzen perforierten Akustikwänden und einem Metallfries aus eloxierten Tafeln auf halber Höhe lässt sich auch für Festveranstaltungen nutzen und ist in beide Richtungen in vier Viertel teilbar. Die Abhängung von Deckenpunktlasten von bis zu 20 Tonnen ist möglich und neueste Konferenztechnik aller Art ist selbstverständlich.

Die um die Hälfte größere und zweifach unterteilbare Halle nebenan hat eher Messestandard und kann auch als reguläre Messehalle genutzt werden. Sie hat an den Längswänden eine Verkleidung aus Akustik-Lochtafeln und an den Stirnseiten verputzte Wände, die nach außen Sichtbeton zeigen. Viel unverkleidete Konstruktion führt zu sparsamer Bauweise, bringt aber erhöhten Planungsaufwand und Schwierigkeiten beim Bau mit sich; was im Rohbau fertig ist, muss vor dem rauen Baubetrieb geschützt werden, denn es ist gleichzeitig Ausbaustandard.

Ein Kongressbetrieb kommt nicht ohne eine umfangreiche Verwaltung, zahlreiche Veranstaltungsbüros, kleinere Besprechungszimmer und Nebenräume aus. Die Büros haben die Architekten in einer Spange an der Westseite vorgesehen. Die Sitzungsräume schweben an der Piazza-Seite in einem Trakt über der Foyerhalle, in engem Kontakt zu Foyer und Sälen. Natürlich kann der Kongressbereich vom Messebetrieb völlig abgekoppelt werden, doch bei Bedarf ist ein sehr enger räumlicher Verbund von Ausstellung, Tagungen und Veranstaltungen möglich.

Access can be controlled with cash desks and barrier systems. After an event, the visitors can leave the hall quickly as the gates on the east side can be opened directly onto the forecourt. Even those events with dense crowds of thousands who all want to leave at the same time will benefit from the convenient location of the multi-storey car park and the high-capacity rapid transit system.

From the shape of hall 1, it is a clear that two suspended roofs as used for the standard halls have been placed together, with a huge main beam replacing the supporting middle wall. In terms of elegance and beauty, this hall compares very favourably with halls of the same size elsewhere.

Meetings and celebrations in the congress centre

However, anyone coming to take part in a conference, listen to a lecture or take part in a large-scale celebration can avoid the centre's entrance hall and go directly to the congress centre. The glass front below the boldly projecting filigree roof is like a shop window displaying the congress goings-on. Along a wide front, the entrances open up into the bright, spacious hall of the foyer. On the left of the transversely arranged foyer, there is the congress room and, on the right, the hall. With its higher-grade fixtures, black, perforated acoustic walls and a metal frieze composed of anodised panels half way up the wall, the congress room can also be used for celebratory events and can be divided into four quarters. Loads of up to 20 metric tons can be suspended from the ceiling and the very latest congress equipment is naturally provided as well.

The hall next door, which is 50% larger, can be divided in two. It has the standard trade fair features and can also be used as a regular trade fair hall. The long walls are covered with perforated acoustic panels whereas the short walls are plastered, showing fair-faced concrete on the outside. A lot of the structural elements are not panelled. This is an economical method of building but involves more planning and difficulties during realisation; the shell of the building has to protected during further work because it is simultaneously the finished condition that will later be visible.

Auf dem Weg zum Auto nach getaner Arbeit ist noch einmal das Prinzip der in die Landschaft eingebundenen Messe zu erleben. Der Messepark setzt sich nach Osten fort, steigt auf dem Rücken des Parkhauses hoch und scheint sich drüben wieder auf die Felder zu senken und sich mit ihnen zu verbinden. Zwischen den beiden Armen des Parkhauses weist die Achse der Messe über die Felder Richtung Osten, mit dem optischen Zielpunkt des Kirchturms von Plieningen.

Parken über der Autobahn

Ein geradezu großstädtisches Gefühl überkommt den Besucher in der schmalen Schlucht zwischen den sechs Geschosse hoch aufragenden Parkhausfronten. Die geschweißten Träger, Streben und Stützen der mächtigen Fachwerkkonstruktion sind von einer Dimension, wie man sie sonst nur in Überseehäfen oder bei Eisenbahnbrücken antrifft, doch die erlebt man normalerweise nur von Weitem. Dem stählernen Konstrukt ist denn auch keinerlei Anmut zu eigen, sondern es bringt kompromisslose Funktionalität zum Ausdruck.

Das Besteigen des Treppenturms oder die Fahrt mit dem Lift bringt den Besucher jedoch auf das oberste Deck in eine andere Welt. Vom Dachgarten aus schweift das Auge über die Filder und, weiter noch, hinüber zum Fernsehturm und übers Land bis hin zur Schwäbischen Alb. Und hier oben erst wird man beim Blick über die Brüstung gewahr, dass man sich über der sechsspurigen, dicht befahrenen Piste der A 8 befindet.

Lohnend ist jedoch auch die Aussicht zurück nach Westen, auf die schwingenden Dächer der Messe, die wie ein Geschwader auf dem Vorfeld bereitzustehen scheinen, um es den Silbervögeln nebenan auf dem Echterdinger Flughafen gleichzutun und in Kürze abzuheben.

A congress facility cannot be operated without extensive administration offices, numerous offices for event organisers, some smaller meeting rooms and auxiliary rooms as well. The architects placed the offices on the west side. The meeting rooms are in a wing on the piazza side and hover over the foyer hall, in close contact with the foyer and large rooms. The congress area can, of course, be completely partitioned off from trade fair operations but, if necessary, exhibitions, conferences and events can be combined with each other in a spatially very intimate arrangement.

On the way to the car after the day's work has been done, the way in which the trade fair centre is embedded in the landscape can be experienced once again. The green strip of the park stretches towards the east, climbs up the rear of the multi-storey car park and, far away, appears to settle back onto and join up with the fields. Between the two arms of the multi-storey car park, the axis of the trade fair centre points over fields towards the east, with the church tower of Plieningen visible in the distance.

Parking above the motorway

In the narrow chasm between the high fronts of the six-level multi-storey car park, the visitor is overcome with a feeling of being in a big city. The welded beams, struts and supports of the huge framework construction are of a size usually encountered only in overseas ports or where there are railway bridges and, even then, are usually seen only from a long way away. Accordingly, the steel structure has nothing graceful about it, being the uncompromising expression of its intended functionality.

After climbing the stairs or using the lift to get to the top floor, however, the visitor enters a completely different world. From the roof garden, the eye sweeps over the fields as far as the television tower and even further across the landscape to the Schwäbischer Alb. And, here at the top, a look over the parapet reveals that one is standing above the busy six lanes of the A8 motorway.

But it is also worthwhile taking a look towards the west, at the sweeping curved roofs of the trade fair centre, which seem to stand ready like a squadron of planes, prepared to take off at a moment's notice like the silver aircraft of Stuttgart airport just a short distance away.

Congresscenter
Glasfront

Congress centre
glassfront

Parkhaus Südseite

South side of the
multi-storey car park

Parkhaus
Multi-storey
car park

Parkhaus von Süden

Multi-storey car park
from the south

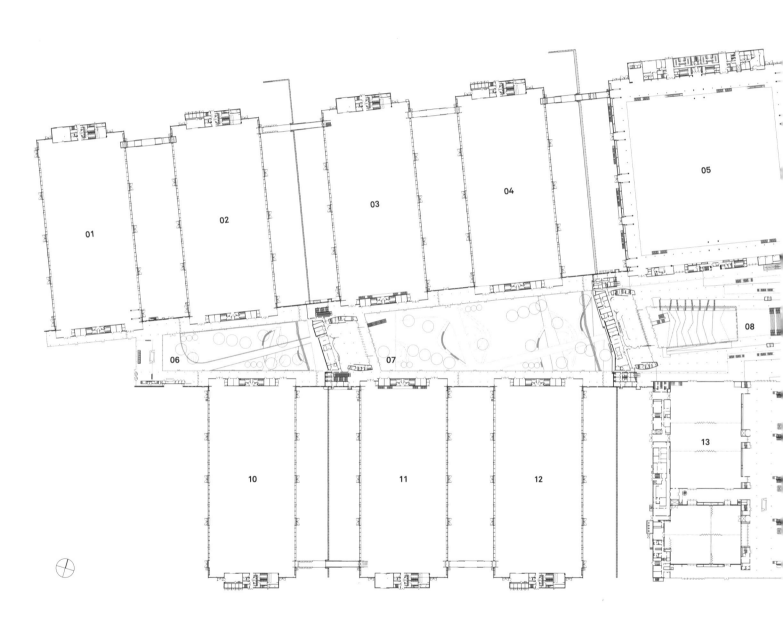

0   100 m

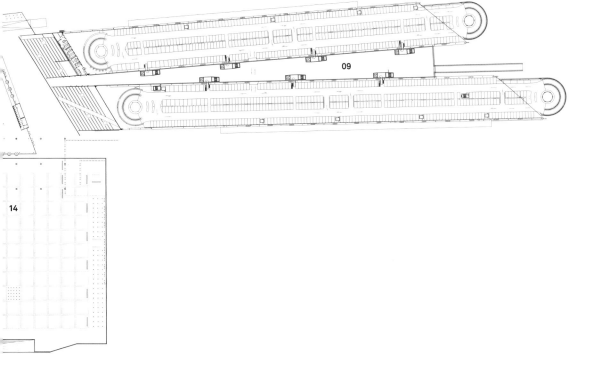

Gesamtansicht Nord	01 Halle 9	Total View Defined to North	01 Hall 9	0	50 m

**Gesamtansicht
Nord**

Maßstab 1:1750

01 Halle 9
08 Eingang Ost
10 Halle 8
11 Halle 6
12 Halle 4
13 ICS Internationales
   Congresscenter
   Stuttgart

**Total View
Defined to North**

Scale 1:1750

01 Hall 9
08 Entrance East
10 Hall 8
11 Hall 6
12 Hall 4
13 ICS International
   Congress Center
   Stuttgart

0   50 m

01   10   11

**Gesamtansicht
Süd**

Maßstab 1:1750

01 Halle 9
02 Halle 7
03 Halle 5
04 Halle 3
05 Halle 1

**Total View
Defined to South**

Scale 1:1750

01 Hall 9
02 Hall 7
03 Hall 5
04 Hall 3
05 Hall 1

0   50 m

05   04

12   13   08

03   02   01

Messerundgang

Längsschnitt
Nord

Maßstab 1:1750

01 Halle 9
02 Halle 7
03 Halle 5
04 Halle 3
05 Halle 1

Inner Round Tour

Long Section
North

Scale 1:1750

01 Hall 9
02 Hall 7
03 Hall 5
04 Hall 3
05 Hall 1

0   50 m

01   02   03

Messerundgang

Längsschnitt
Süd

Maßstab 1:1750

06 Eingang West
08 Eingang Ost
10 Halle 8
11 Halle 6
12 Halle 4

Inner Round Tour

Long Section
South

Scale 1:1750

06 Entrance West
08 Entrance East
10 Hall 8
11 Hall 6
12 Hall 4

0   50 m

08   12

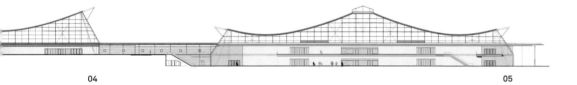

04   05

11   10   06

Eingang Ost

Ansicht
Osten

Maßstab 1:1500

Entrance East

Eastern
View

Scale 1:1500

Eingang Ost

Ebene
Erdgeschoss

Maßstab 1:1500

Entrance East

Ground Floor
Level

Scale 1:1500

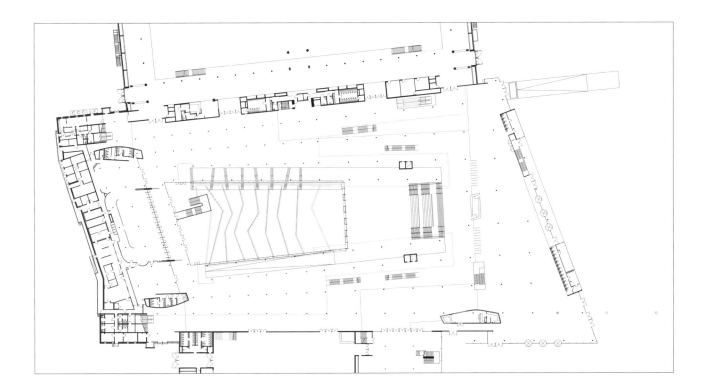

0   50 m

Eingang Ost

Längsschnitt

Maßstab 1:1500

Entrance East

Long Section

Scale 1:1500

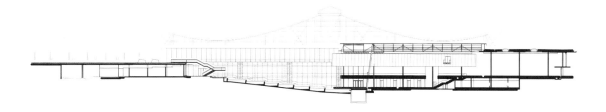

Eingang Ost

Ebene
Obergeschoss

Maßstab 1:1500

Entrance East

Upper Floor
Level

Scale 1:1500

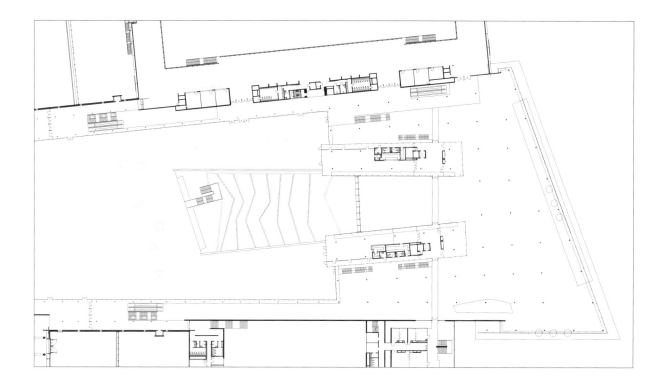

0   50 m

ICS
Internationales
Congresscenter
Stuttgart

ICS
International
Congress Center
Stuttgart

Querschnitt

Cross Section

Maßstab 1:1000

Scale 1:1000

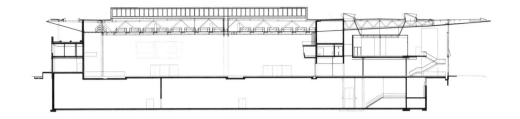

ICS
Internationales
Congresscenter
Stuttgart

ICS
International
Congress Center
Stuttgart

Ebene
Erdgeschoss

Ground Floor
Level

Maßstab 1:1000

Scale 1:1000

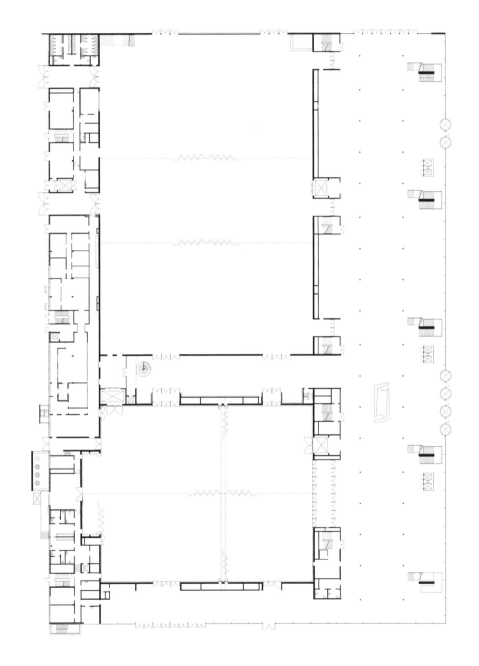

0   50 m

ICS
Internationales
Congresscenter
Stuttgart

ICS
International
Congress Center
Stuttgart

Ebene
Obergeschoss

Upper Floor
Level

Maßstab 1:1000

Scale 1:1000

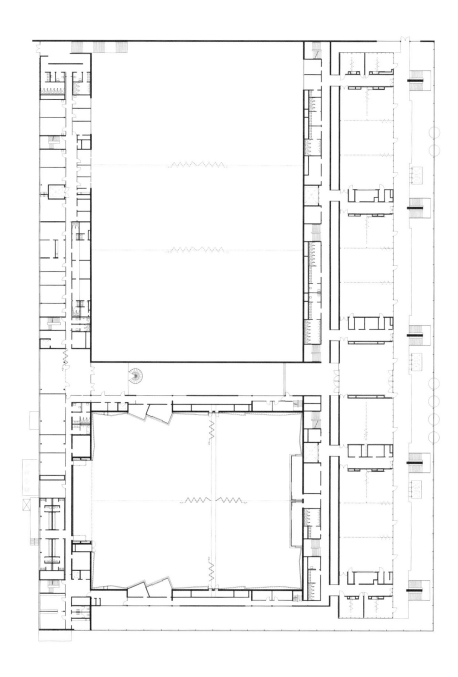

0

50 m

Halle 6

Ebene
Erdgeschoss

Maßstab 1:1000

Hall 6

Ground Floor
Level

Scale 1:1000

0   50 m

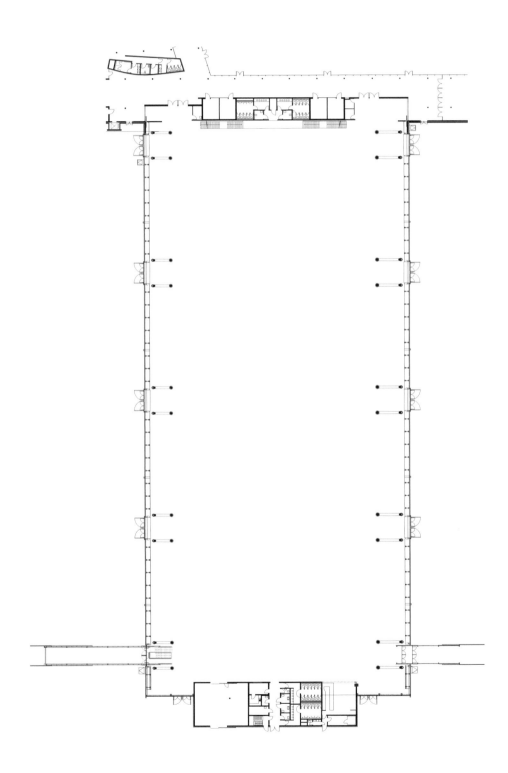

Halle 4

Querschnitt

Maßstab 1:1000

Hall 4

Cross Section

Scale 1:1000

Halle 4

Ebene
Erdgeschoss

Maßstab 1:1000

Hall 4

Ground Floor
Level

Scale 1:1000

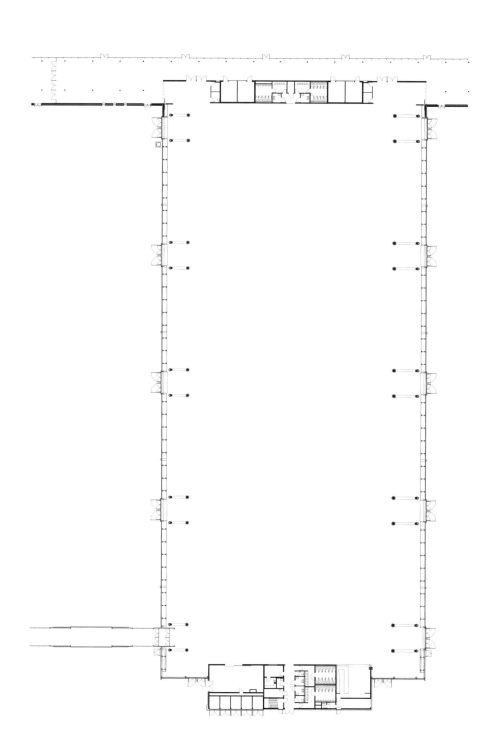

Halle 5

Ansicht
Nord

Maßstab 1:1000

Hall 5

Northern
View

Scale 1:1000

Halle 5

Ansicht
Süd

Maßstab 1:1000

Hall 5

Southern
View

Scale 1:1000

Halle 5

Ebene
Untergeschoss

Maßstab 1:1000

Hall 5

Ground Floor
Level

Scale 1:1000

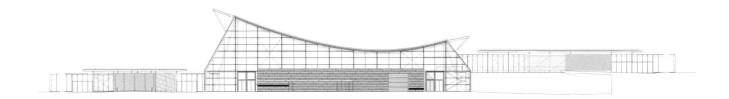

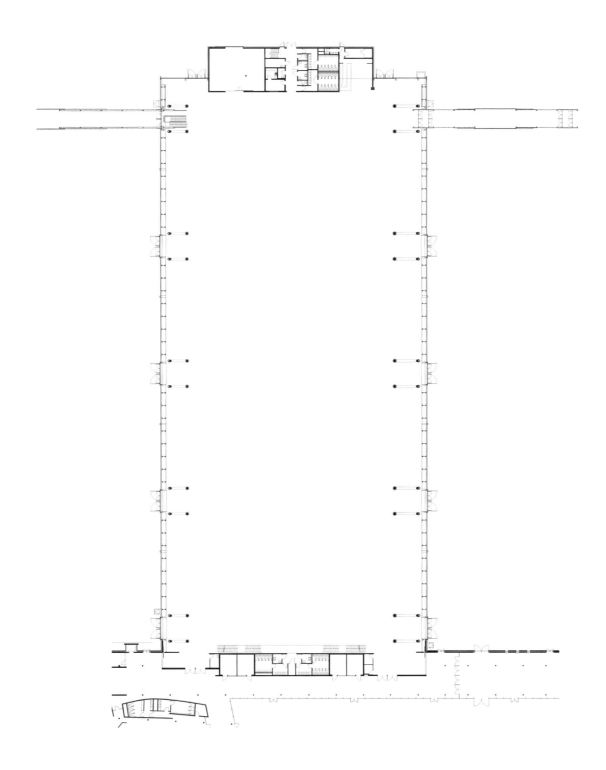

Halle 1

Querschnitt

Maßstab 1:1000

Hall 1

Cross Section

Scale 1:1000

Halle 1

Ansicht
Süd

Maßstab 1:1000

Hall 1

Southern
View

Scale 1:1000

Halle 1

Ebene
Erdgeschoss

Maßstab 1:1000

Hall 1

Ground Floor
Level

Scale 1:1000

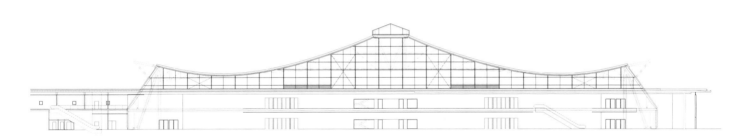

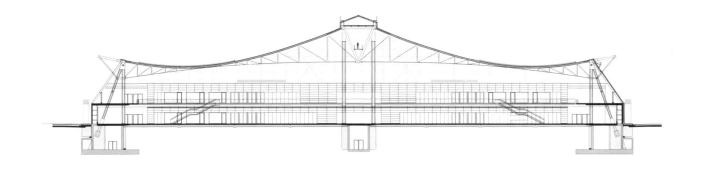

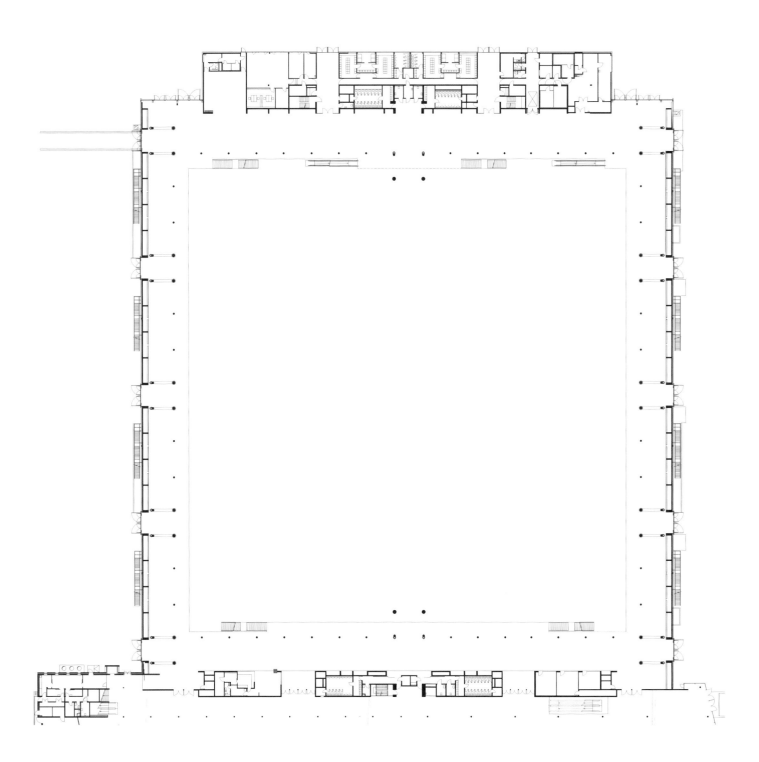

Parkhaus

Parkebene 0

Maßstab 1:1500

Multi-storey car park

Parking Level 0

Scale 1:1500

0   50 m

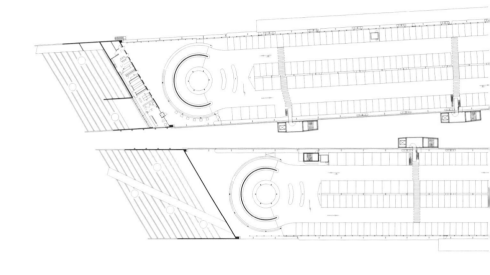

Parkhaus

Dachebene

Maßstab 1:1500

Multi-storey car park

Roof Level

Scale 1:1500

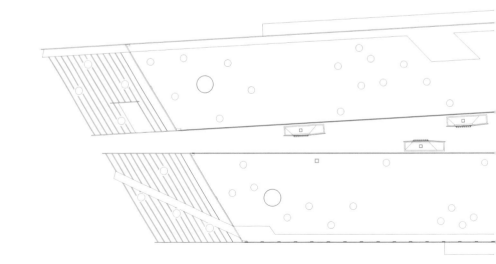

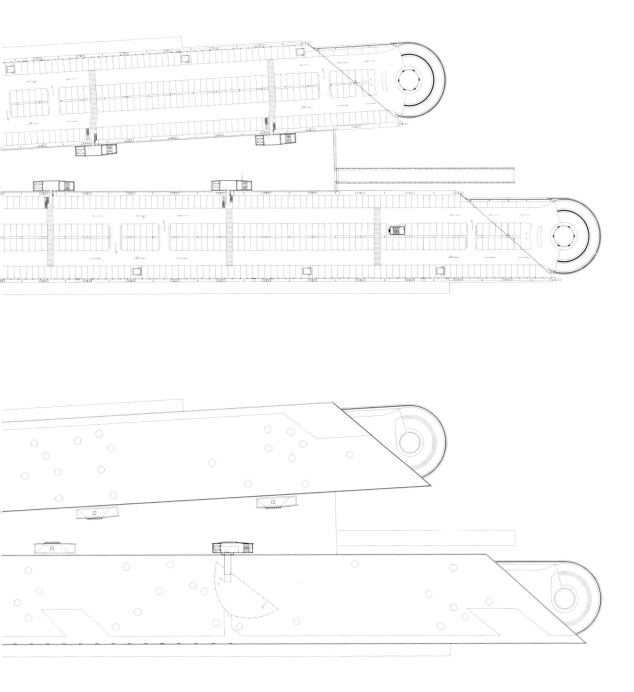

Parkhaus
Nordspange

Ansicht
Süd

Maßstab 1:1500

Multi-storey car park
North Clip

Southern
View

Scale 1:1500

0   50 m

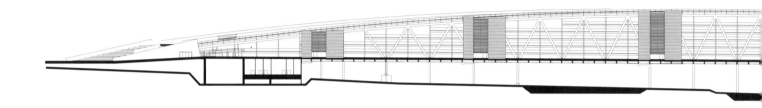

Parkhaus
Südspange

Ansicht
Süd

Maßstab 1:1500

Multi-storey car park
South Clip

Southern
View

Scale 1:1500

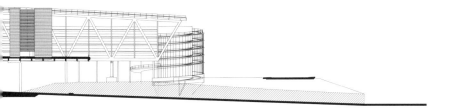

Seite 158–159
Lageplan des Messegeländes
mit Grünplanung und Verkehrsführung

Maßstab 1:4500

Page 158–159
Location diagram of the trade fair site
with green area plan and transport routes

Scale 1:4500

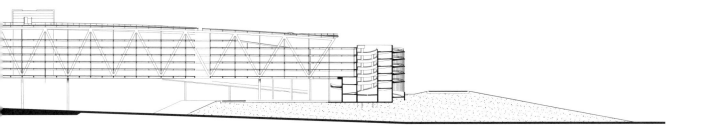

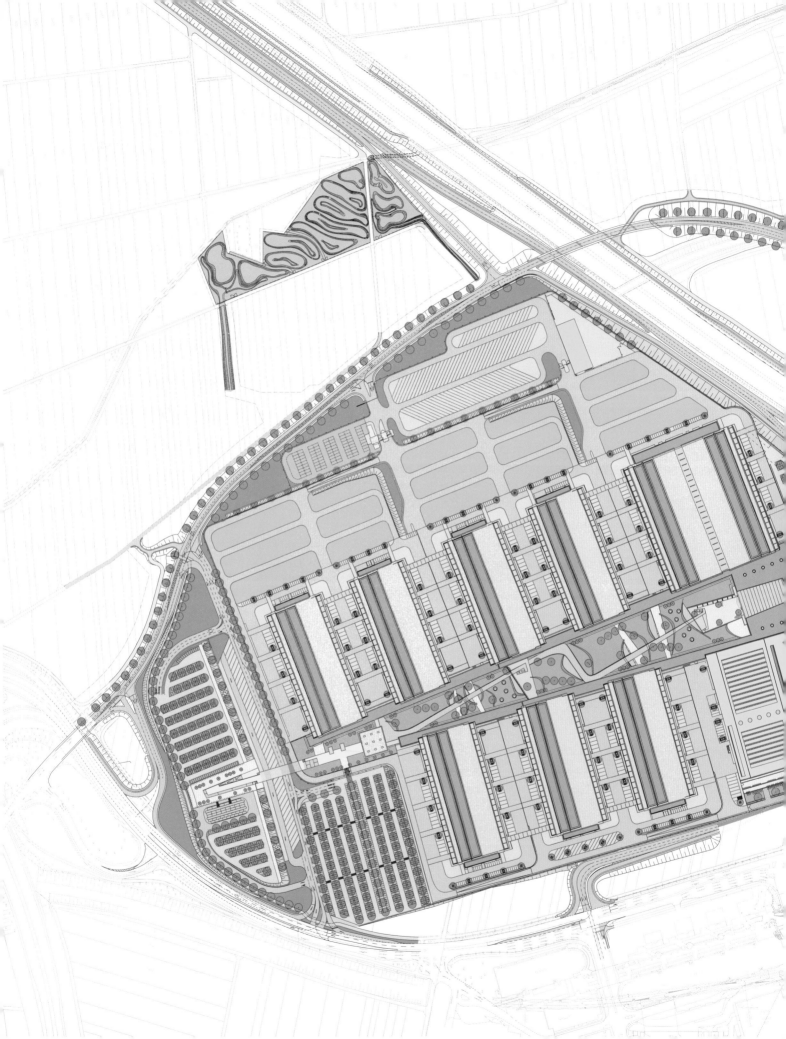

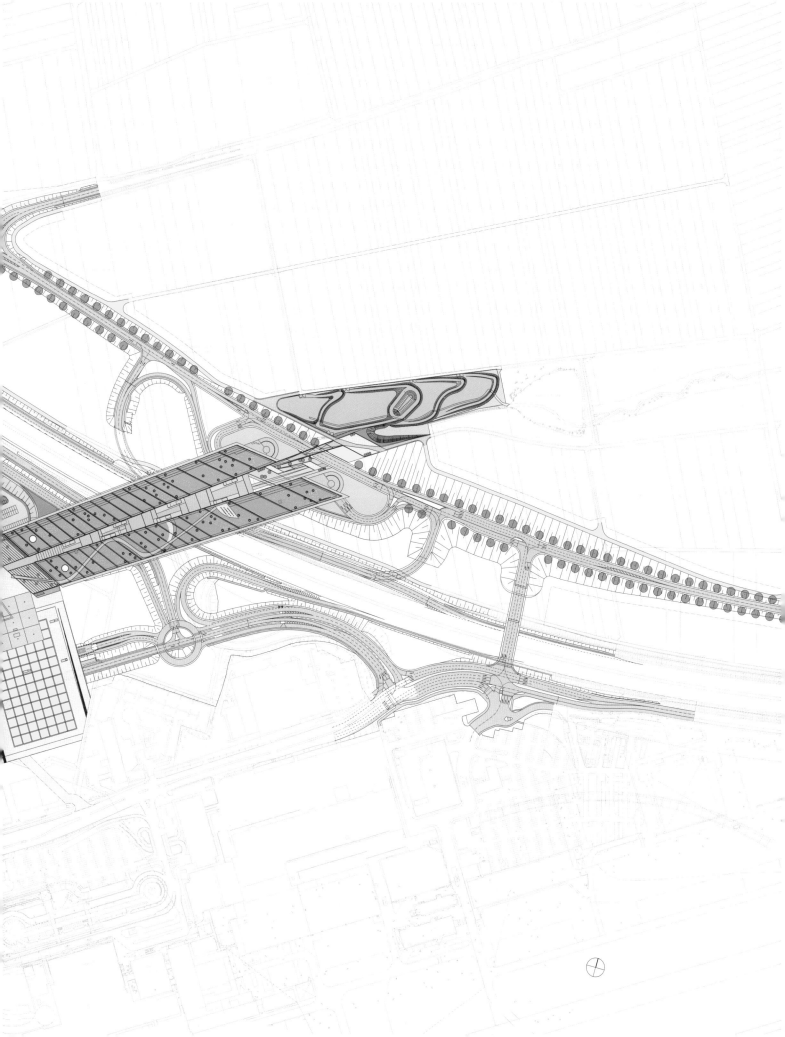

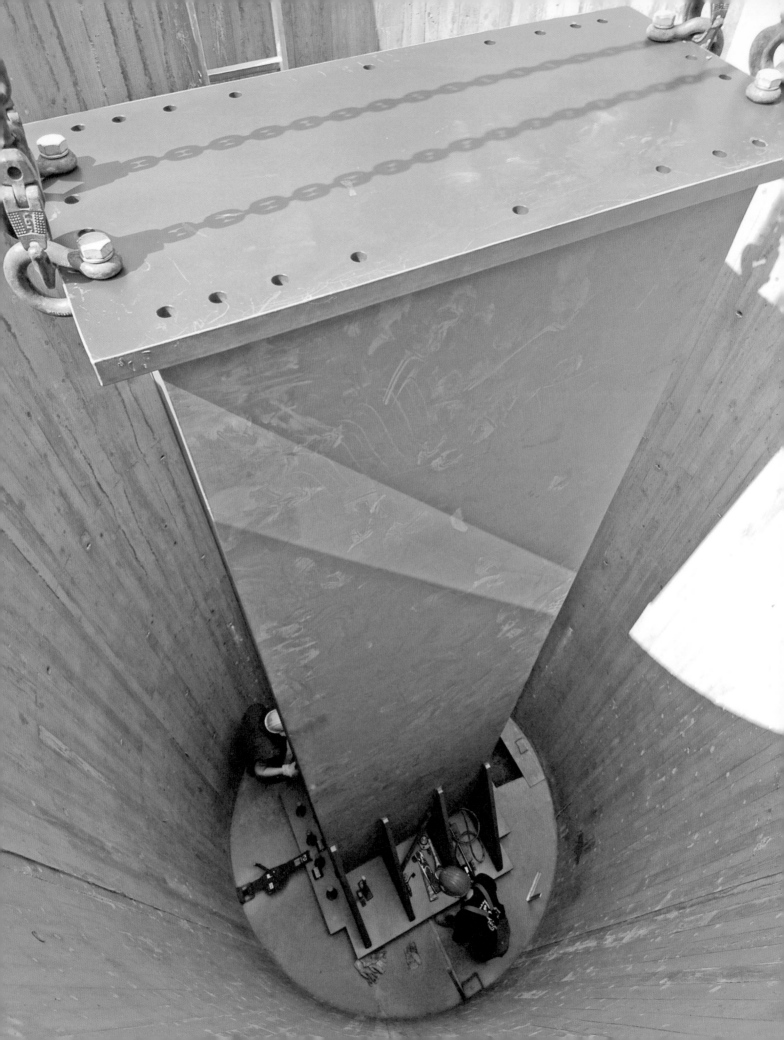

**Tragen und Lasten –
Die Konstruktion**

Die zeichenhaften Bauten
der Neuen Messe Stuttgart
sind auf ungewöhnliche
bautechnische Weise ent-
standen

**Loads and load bearers –
The structural engineering**

The method of construction
used for the emblematic
buildings of the New Stuttgart
Trade Fair Centre was
unusual to say the least.

Tragen und Lasten –
Die Konstruktion
Die zeichenhaften Bauten der Neuen Messe Stuttgart sind auf ungewöhnliche bautechnische Weise entstanden

Loads and load bearers –
The structural engineering
The method of construction used for the emblematic buildings of the New Stuttgart Trade Fair Centre was unusual to say the least.

Schon beim Anflug auf den Flughafen in Leinfelden-Echterdingen prägt sich das Bild von einer Landschaft beschwingter Dächer ein. Das liegt an den unverwechselbaren Bauformen der acht Messehallen. Hinzu kommt das eindrucksvolle Parkhaus, das mit zwei riesigen Fingern über die Autobahn greift und für alle Autofahrer auf der A 8 zur Landmarke geworden ist. Bauwerke in diesem zyklopischen Maßstab wollen gestalterisch bewältigt sein, sind aber auch eine Herausforderung für die Ingenieure. Sowohl die signifikanten Hallen wie auch die ungewöhnlichen Parkhausbrücken sind auf besondere bautechnische Weise zustande gekommen.

Die dynamische Form der Messehallen ergibt sich aus den selten anzutreffenden Hängedächern. Man denkt an die artverwandte Halle 26 auf der Hannover Messe, die der Architekt Thomas Herzog 1996 mit den Ingenieuren Schlaich Bergermann und Partner realisierte. Das Konstrukt mit den konkaven, durchhängenden Dachflächen gilt als besonders materialsparend, da der Stahl des Tragwerks viel bereitwilliger Zugkräfte als Druck oder Biegung aufnimmt und dabei mit weit geringeren Querschnitten auskommt. Wenn diese Bauweise dennoch wenig Verbreitung gefunden hat, so deshalb, weil das Hängedach flexibel und recht bewegungsfreudig ist, was Probleme bei Wind- und Schneelasten, beim Anschluss anderer Bauteile und bei der Montage mit sich bringt.

Besonders die Bauphase hält für die Ingenieure von Mayr + Ludescher knifflige Fragen bereit. Statt von mächtigen Fachwerkträgern, die man konventionell per Kran versetzen kann, werden die 70 Meter breiten Hallen von dünnen Stahlbändern überspannt, die in einer flachen Parabelkurve durchhängen. Die Tragbänder bestehen aus gerade mal 15 Zentimeter hohen und 25 Zentimeter breiten H-Profilen (deren Trägheitsmoment ist in beiden Achsen gleich, um Ausweichtorsion zu verhindern). Da die Bänder unterschiedlich durchhängen, hat jedes eine andere Geometrie. Die Profile wurden deshalb im Werk vorgekrümmt, in vier Teilen angeliefert und vor Ort zu ganzer Länge zusammengeschweißt. Ihre präzise Endform erhalten sie durch Biegung unter Last. Das Problem ist nun, dass sich die Hängebänder während der Montage des Dachs unsymmetrisch durchbiegen wie eine Wäscheleine, bei der man an einem Ende mit dem Anklammern der Wäschestücke anfängt. Hier kann man sich mit Ballastsäcken, mit

Seen from a plane on its descent to the airport in Leinfelden-Echterdingen, a landscape of sweeping roofs presents itself to the eye. This is due to the unmistakable shape of the eight trade fair halls. There is also the impressive multi-storey car park which stretches its two huge »fingers« over the motorway and, in the meantime, has become a landmark for all drivers on the A8. Building on this titanic scale is an enormous challenge for both designers and engineers. In this case, the striking halls and the unusual bridges of the multi-storey car park required a special structural engineering approach to their construction and design.

The dynamic shape of the halls in the trade fair centre derives from the rarely encountered hanging roofs. They are reminiscent of hall 26 at the Hanover trade fair centre which architect Thomas Herzog and engineers Schlaich Bergermann und Partner created in 1996. The structure with the concave sagging roofs is regarded as an especially effective way of saving money on materials as the steel of the load-bearing structure is much better at absorbing tensile forces than the forces exerted by pressure or bending. Its cross-sections, as a result, can be much smaller as well. Nevertheless, this structural design is by no means widespread because such a suspended roof tends to move about a lot. This causes problems when it is windy or snows, when other parts have to be connected and when it is actually being assembled.

For the engineers of Mayr + Ludescher, the construction phase was especially problematic. Instead of heavy girders which can be conventionally moved around with cranes, there are thin steel strips that span the 70 metre-wide halls and hang down in a smooth parabolic curve. These load-bearing strips are made of only 15 centimetre-high and 25 centimetre-wide H sections (their moment of inertia is the same on both axes in order to prevent yield torsion). As the depth of sagging varies from strip to strip, each one has its own particular geometry. Each section was therefore bent in a curve in advance in the factory. It was then delivered in four parts, and finally welded together on site. The precise final shape results from bending under load. The problem was that, when the roof was being fitted, the suspended strips sagged unsymmetrically like a washing line where wash-

Seite 160
Pendelstützen mit in Betonschächten tiefliegenden Fußpunkten tragen die Parkhausbrücken

Page 160
Articulated columns with bases inserted into deep concrete shafts support the bridges of the multi-storey car park

01 Querschnitt Tragsystem der Standardhallen mit an der Unterseite abgespanntem Hängeband, Stützbock und Zugverankerung im Untergrund

Cross-section of the load-bearing system for the standard halls with a hanging tie attached underneath plus trestle and tie rod anchor in the substrate

02 Die parabolisch gebogenen Hängebänder auf der Baustelle

The parabolic hanging ties on the construction site

03 Verankerung der Zugstrebe des Stützbocks im Fundamentblock

Anchoring of the diagonal ties of the trestle in the foundation block

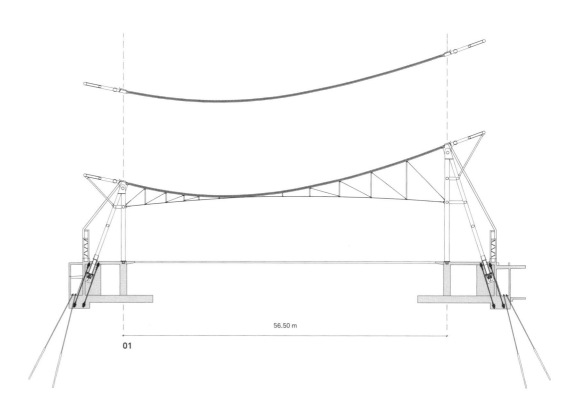

56.50 m

01

02

03

Seite 164–165
Stahlbau ist Millimeterarbeit
auch bei der Montage

Page 164–165
In steel construction, great
precision is essential,
especially during assembly

01–02 Ballastsäcke während der Montage
der Hallendächer

Sacks of ballast used when the
hall roofs were fitted

03 Beplankung der Trapezblechdeckung mit
einer Feinblechauflage

Attachment of thin metal sheeting on
the metal-sheeting cover which features
trapezoidal corrugations

04 Montage der Trapezblechdeckung
(Seite 168–169)

Attachment of the metal-sheeting cover
with its trapezoidal corrugations
(Page 168–169)

01

02

03

04

Schotter gefüllten BigPacks, behelfen. Mit deren Hilfe wurde schon in der Montagephase die endgültige Belastung simuliert, wodurch die Bänder gleich in ihre endgültige Form kamen. Mit dem Fortschreiten der Dachmontage und damit der Auflast wurden die Säcke unter ständiger messtechnischer Überwachung der Dachgeometrie Stück für Stück abgehängt. Dadurch konnten die Bänder ihre Form beibehalten. Das Ballastmaterial wurde übrigens nicht wieder mühsam abtransportiert, sondern an Ort und Stelle als Unterbau für den Hallenboden einplaniert.

Eleganz der Konstruktion

Weil das Regenwasser zu den Giebelseiten hin ablaufen soll, sind die mittleren Bänder 50 Zentimeter kürzer und somit flacher gespannt als die stärker durchhängenden Randbänder, wodurch das Dach zusätzlich zu der konkaven in Querrichtung eine konvexe Wölbung in Längsrichtung erhielt.

Als Dachkonstruktion wurden quer auf die tragenden Bänder Trapezbleche montiert, Blechtafeln mit 16 Zentimeter hohen trapezförmigen Rippen. Wegen der Dachneigung in Querrichtung mussten die Trapezbleche im Mittelteil gestaucht und in der Randzone gereckt werden, um die 50 Zentimeter Differenz auszugleichen. Nach ihrer Montage wurde noch eine Schicht Feinblech aufgenietet. So konnte sowohl auf Pfetten (Querträger) wie auch auf Diagonalversteifungen verzichtet werden und es blieb bei der extrem geringen Stärke von 31 Zentimetern für die 10.000 Quadratmeter große Dachkonstruktion. Die Unterspannungen durch dünne Drahtseile gegen windbedingte Schwingungen fallen in der Halle nicht ins Auge und tun der Eleganz der feingliedrigen, an eine Zeltbahn erinnernden Konstruktion keinen Abbruch. Auch bei den Details, den Anschlüssen, Knoten und Seilverbindungen haben die Ingenieure mit eleganten Lösungen Neuerungen eingeführt.

ing is hung on the line starting at one end. The remedy adopted was to use Big Packs, sacks filled with ballast. During the assembly phase, this made it possible to simulate the final load to give the strips their final shape. As fitting of the roof progressed and the load increased, the sacks were detached one by one while the roof geometry was continuously monitored with measuring instruments. As a result, the strips were able to retain their shape. Incidentally, the ballast material did not have to be taken away, but was used on site as the substructure for the hall floors.

Structural elegance

Because rainwater is intended to flow towards the gable ends, the strips in the middle are 50 centimetres shorter and therefore do not hang down as much as the longer ones at the edges. This makes the roof concave in a transverse direction but gives it a convex uplift when seen longitudinally.

Trapezoidal metal sheets in the form of sheet-metal panels with 16 centimetre-high trapezoidal ribs were mounted transversely on the load-bearing strips to form the structure of the roof. Due to the transverse slope of the roof, the trapezoidal metal plates had to be compressed in the middle and stretched out at the edges in order to make up for the 50 centimetre difference. After they were fitted, a layer of final metal sheeting was riveted on. It was therefore possible to do without purlins (cross-beams) and diagonal reinforcing elements; the very small thickness of 31 centimetres was retained for the entire roof structure, which is 10,000 square metres in size. The underlay sections in the form of thin wire cables to prevent vibration caused by wind are inconspicuous in the hall and do not detract from the elegance of the fine structure, which is reminiscent of a tarpaulin. In the details such as the connection points, nodes and cables as well, the engineers introduced a variety of elegant solutions.

However, a price has to be paid for the suspended roof construction: the low weight means that the horizontal loads are much smaller but suspension of the roof involves considerable horizontal forces which have to be coped with. Massive steel-tube trestles are therefore used to counter the tension and transfer 1500 metric tons of tensile force into the ground by means of 40 ground ties.

Einen Preis hat die Hängedachkonstruktion allerdings: Das geringere Gewicht bringt zwar wesentlich kleinere Horizontallasten mit sich, doch sind aus der Dachspannung erhebliche Horizontalkräfte abzutragen. Mächtige Stahlrohrböcke stemmen sich deshalb gegen die Spannung und bringen 1500 Tonnen Zugkräfte mittels 40 Erdankern in den Boden.

Bei der Hochhalle mit der doppelten Grundfläche wurden einfach zwei Hängedächer aneinandergesetzt. Dazu war dann doch in der Hallenmitte ein Träger aus Stahlrohrfachwerk notwendig, der mit 168 Meter Länge, einer Höhe von neun Metern und mit 800 Tonnen Gewicht Eindruck macht. Zum Zusammenschweißen wurde extra eine Umhausung gebaut, um unter Werkstattbedingungen arbeiten zu können. Beim Hochhieven des 170 Tonnen schweren südlichen Teilstücks gab es einen Unfall, bei dem ein Kranführer sein Leben verlor. Das havarierte Teil musste sorgfältig geprüft und vermessen werden, hatte aber beim Absturz keinen Schaden genommen und konnte schließlich montiert werden.

Zwei Brücken kommen in Bewegung

Nicht unelegant, wenn auch ungleich massiver tritt östlich anschließend das Parkhaus der Messe in Erscheinung. Die Architekten hatten ursprünglich eine leichtere Seilkonstruktion vorgeschlagen, doch das Stahlfachwerk erwies sich als wirtschaftlicher. Auch und vor allem wegen der Autobahn. Denn die gewichtige Frage war: Wie baut man ein sechsgeschossiges Parkhaus bei laufendem Verkehr über eine der meistbefahrenen Autobahnen Deutschlands? Leonhardt, Andrä und Partner, die Ingenieure des Bauwerks, sind nicht von ungefähr als Brückenbauspezialisten bekannt und es war Professor Fritz Leonhardt, der das inzwischen international eingesetzte »Taktschiebeverfahren« für den Brückenbau entwickelt hat.

60 Meter in 15 Stunden, das Tempo ist nicht beeindruckend, indes handelt es sich um ein »Fahrzeug« von 3840 Tonnen Gewicht. Genauer gesagt um einen Schlitten, denn das auf der Plieninger Seite zusammengeschweißte Brückenteil glitt, durch Hydraulikpressen bewegt, auf Teflonplatten über die 27 Stützen und kragte frei über die achtspurige Autopiste, bis es auf den Stützen jenseits der Autobahn auflag.

For the high hall with its double green area, two hanging roofs were simply placed together. To do this, it was necessary to place a beam made of latticed steel tubes in the middle of the hall. 168 metres long, nine metres high and weighing 800 metric tons, it is a highly impressive piece of work. In order to weld it together, a special enclosure had to be built so that work could be done under conditions similar to those in a workshop. When the southern section, weighing 170 metric tons, was being lifted, there was an unfortunate accident causing the crane driver to lose his life. The section which had been dropped had to be carefully inspected and measured but had not been damaged by the fall and was finally fitted in place.

Two bridges on the move

By no means inelegant although incomparably more massive, the multi-storey car park puts in an appearance in the east part of the site. The architects had originally proposed a lighter cable construction but the steel framework method turned out to be more economical. Also and primarily because of the motorway. The central question was: How can a six-level multi-storey car park be built without stopping the traffic on one of the busiest motorways in Germany? Leonhardt, Andrä and Partner, the engineers, are not known as bridge building specialists without reason and it was Professor Fritz Leonhardt who developed the »timed-shifting« method for bridge construction which is now used internationally.

The speed is not impressive, being only 60 metres in 15 hours, but it must be borne in mind that the »vehicle« in this case weighed 3840 metric tons. To be more precise, it was a sledge-like structure. After being welded together on the Plieningen side, the bridge section was moved by hydraulic presses causing it to slide on Teflon plates over the 27 supports until it came to rest on the supports on the other side of the motorway.

01 Querschnitt der Hochhalle mit Mittelträger und gespiegelten Hängedächern

Cross-section of the high hall with centre girder and suspended roofs

02 Zusammenschweißen der Mittelträger der Hochhalle in Schutzeinhausung

Centre girders of the high hall being welded together in a protective shed

03–04 Montage des 800 Tonnen schweren Mittelträgers der Hochhalle mit Schwerlastkränen

Centre girder, weighing 800 metric tons, being mounted in the high hall with heavy lift cranes

Seite 172–173
Die Parkhausbrücken über die Autobahn nach der Verschiebephase

Page 172–173
The bridges of the multi-storey car park over the motorway after being moved into position

01

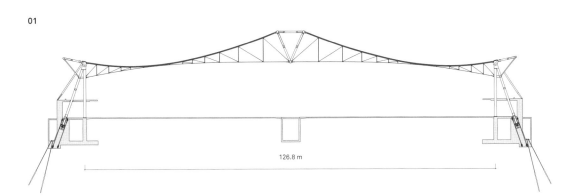

126.8 m

02

03

04

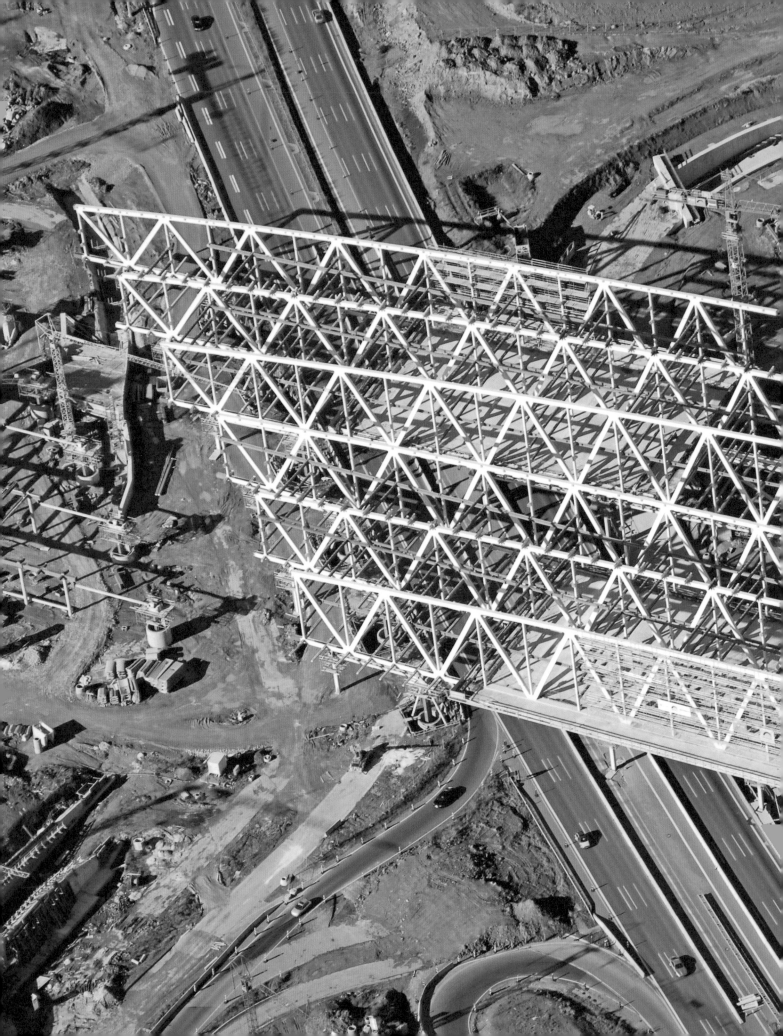

01 Montage der Brückenteile des Parkhauses
vor dem Verschieben

Assembly of the various parts of the bridges
belonging to the multi-storey car park
before bridges were moved into position

02 Verbindungsweg zwischen den beiden
Parkhausbrücken

Connecting pathway between the two
bridges of the multi-storey car park

03 Blick in eine Wendelrampe
des Parkhauses

View into a spiral staircase of the
multi-storey car park

04 Montierte Brückenteile vor der Verschiebung
über die Autobahn

Assembled bridge parts before being moved
into position over the motorway

01

02

03
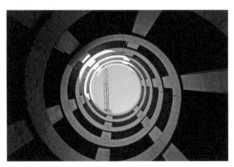

04

Doch zunächst mussten die Brückenteile montiert werden. Die haushohen Fachwerkträger, jeweils drei pro Brücke, bestehen aus geschweißten, im Querschnitt 80 mal 60 Zentimeter starken Hohlkastenprofilen. Bis zur noch transportierbaren Größe waren die Teile im Werk hergestellt worden. Auf der Baustelle wurden die Fachwerkträger liegend zusammengesetzt, verschweißt und dann erst aufgerichtet und mit den Querrahmen zum biegesteifen räumlichen Fachwerk (Chassis) verbunden.

Drei Schübe waren notwendig, jeweils mit Zusammenbau der Chassis, Verschub, Anbau des nächsten »Schusses«, Verschub usw., bis die Autobahn überbrückt war und die beiden Endstücke an Ort und Stelle ergänzt sowie die Anbindung an die Zufahrtspindeln als Festpunkte auf der Messeseite fixiert werden konnten. An der Ostseite docken die beiden Brücken an die Betonspindeln mit in der Längsrichtung beweglichen querfesten Führungslagern an.

Der Fachwerkteil des südlichen Brückenfingers, ein 246 Meter langer Stahlkoloss von 35 Meter Breite und 22 Meter Höhe, ist das bislang größte Bauteil, das mit dieser Technik in seine endgültige Position bugsiert wurde.

Eine Besonderheit ist der feuersichere »Autobahndeckel«, die Decke direkt über der A 8 mit beiderseits fünf Meter Auskragung. Oberhalb gilt der Bau als offenes Parkhaus und muss nur 30 Minuten Feuer überstehen. Der Deckel soll das Bauwerk bei einer Brandkatastrophe auf der Autobahn 90 Minuten von unten schützen. Die Hauptstützen müssen gar 120 Minuten Befeuerung widerstehen. Auch ein ICE-Unfall wie in Eschede wird den Bau nicht gefährden können.

Der weitere Ausbau ist dagegen Routine: Einbau der Zwischendecken, weitgehend mit dem stahlbauadäquat rasch zu montierenden Hoesch-Additiv-Deckensystem (Stahltrapezprofile mit Aufbeton) ausgeführt, der Rampen und Treppenhäuser, Endanstrich, Installationen aller Art, Montage des Verkehrsleitsystems und schließlich Aufbringen der Erdschicht und der Bepflanzung auf dem Dach.

Wie meist bei exzellenter Arbeit der Ingenieure sieht das Ergebnis recht »einfach« aus und lässt kaum mehr erahnen, wie viele Alternativen bedacht, wie viele Bauteile berechnet und wie vielen Vorschriften Rechnung getragen werden musste, bis dem Bauherrn der Schlüssel (in diesem Fall der zur Einfahrtschranke) übergeben werden konnte.

First of all however, the parts of the bridge had to be assembled. The house-high lattice-type beams, three for each bridge, are made of welded hollow box sections measuring 80 by 60 centimetres. Parts that could be transported had been made in the factory. On the building site, the lattice-type beams were joined together, welded and only then raised and connected to the cross frames to form a rigid, chassis structure.

Three pushes were necessary; assembly of the chassis, push, attachment of the next section, push, and so on until the structure spanned the motorway. The end pieces were then added and fastened to the abutment posts as fixed points on the side of the trade fair centre. On the east side, the two bridges »dock onto« the concrete posts with the guide bearings which are movable in the longitudinal direction but fixed in the transverse direction.

The chassis part of the southern bridge, a 246 metre-long steel colossus with a width of 35 metres and a height of 22 metres, is the largest single item that has ever been moved into its final position with this method.

A special feature is the fire-proof »motorway cover«, the deck directly above the A8 which extends outwards by five meters on each side. Above this, the structure is an open multi-storey car park and must be able to withstand fire for only 30 minutes. The »cover« is intended to protect the building for 90 minutes in the event of a fire on the motorway. The main supports must even be able to withstand 120 minutes of fire. Even an ICE accident like the one in Eschede would not be able to endanger the building.

The remaining finishing work was routine: installation of the intermediate ceilings, mostly done with the Hoesch additive ceiling system (trapezoidal steel sections with concrete topping) which is suitable for steel structures, then the ramps and stairwells, the paintwork, all kinds of wiring and cables, installation of the traffic control system and finally application of a layer of soil for the plants on the roof.

As is usually the case when engineers do excellent work, the result seems very »simple« and hardly gives a hint of how many alternatives have been considered, how many parts have to be calculated and how many regulations have to be complied with before the client can be given the key (in this case to the entrance barrier).

**Jahreszeiten
aus dem Rechner**
> Das avancierte Energie-
> management sorgt
> für ungewöhnlich günstige
> Betriebskosten

**Seasons from
the computer**
> The advanced energy
> management system
> ensures unusually low
> operating costs.

Jahreszeiten aus dem Rechner
Das avancierte Energiemanagement sorgt für ungewöhnlich günstige Betriebskosten

Seasons from the computer
The advanced energy management system ensures unusually low operating costs.

Wie spart man eine Million Kubikmeter Lüftung pro Stunde? Diese seltsame Frage kann Michael Bauer von DS-Plan beantworten. Die Drees & Sommer-Tochter war schon in der Optimierungsphase der drei Wettbewerbsersten zur Beratung in Sachen Systemplanung der technischen Grundkonzeption hinzugezogen worden und betreute nach der Entscheidung die beauftragten Architekten. Dazu gehörten die Konzeption der gebäudetechnischen Ausrüstung und die Betreuung der Ausschreibungen für die Fachplanung. Bis alle an die 100 Fachplaner an Bord waren, diente DS-Plan als »Sparringspartner« für die Architekten und gleichzeitig als Bindeglied zur Messegesellschaft, indem es mit den Messebetreibern den Bedarf an Energie- und Medienversorgung für die Hallen ermittelte und in den Planungsprozess einbrachte.

Schließlich wurde DS-Plan auch noch in der Bauphase mit dem speziellen Verfahren der »Emulation« aktiv. Bei diesem Verfahren werden die von den Firmen zum Einbau vorgesehenen Mess-Steuer-Regelelemente der haustechnischen Anlagen an einen Rechner der DS-Plan angeschlossen, der den Messebetrieb simuliert, ob Sommer oder Winter, ob Tag oder Nacht, ob Hochbetrieb oder verhaltener Geschäftsverlauf. Die Jahreszeiten finden also schon vor dem reellen Betrieb im Rechner statt und diese virtuellen Szenarien müssen die Aggregate und Steuerungen meistern. Wie man am Flugsimulator Flugstunden spart, spart man bei der Emulation Einfahrzeiten der Messe und damit jede Menge Ärger und Euro.

Während die Versorgung der Messestände mit Strom und Informationsmedien, mit Datenautobahnen und WLAN schlicht den international neuesten Standards entsprechend geplant wurde, stellten Lüftung, Heizung und Kühlung für die Planer die eigentliche Problematik dar. Für Zehntausende von Quadratmetern Hallenfläche müssen große Energiemengen bereitgestellt werden – und das nur an wenigen Tagen im Jahr, denn von den 80 bis 120 Messetagen sind nur wenige sehr kalt und nur wenige sehr warm. Der Kongressbetrieb kommt ebenfalls auf höchstens 180 Tage im Jahr, wobei die Kapazität selten ausgelastet ist. Die Herausforderung war also, hohe Spitzenlasten kurzfristig abdecken zu können, was die Haustechniker gemeinhin nicht in Begeisterung ausbrechen lässt.

How do you reduce the amount of air needed for ventilation by one million cubic metres per hour? This strange question can be answered by Michael Bauer from DS-Plan. The Drees & Sommer subsidiary had already been engaged in the refining phase of the three competition winners to provide advice on system planning for the underlying technical concept and support the architects after the jury had reached their final verdict. This included preparation of a concept for the building systems equipment and the provision of support in the invitation for bids for the specialist planning. Until all 100 specialist planners were on board, DS-Plan was used as a »sparring partner« for the architects and simultaneously acted as a link to the company responsible for the trade fair centre. It did this by working with the operators of the trade fair centre to determine the energy and media requirements for the halls and to incorporate these requirements in the ongoing planning process.

Finally, DS-Plan also took part in the construction phase by assuming responsibility for the special »emulation« process. This method involves connecting the in-house measuring and control equipment envisaged by the companies for installation to a DS-Plan computer which simulates trade fair operations whether it is summer or winter, day or night, busy or quiet. The seasons are thus emulated in the computer before any real trade fair activities take place. The various items of building-systems equipment and control devices must be able to cope with these virtual scenarios. Just as hours of flying can be avoided with the help of a flight simulator, the emulation saves time preparing for trade fair activities and, besides cutting down on costs, avoids a great many annoying problems.

Whereas supplying the trade fair stands with electricity and information as well as with data highways and WLAN was planned without fuss according to the latest international standards, ventilation, heating and cooling were the real problems for the planners. For tens of thousands of square metres of hall space, large amounts of energy have to be provided – and this has to be done on just a few days in the year given that only a

Seite 176
Befahrbare Medienkanäle verbinden alle Hallen
mit der Technikzentrale

Page 176
Passageways in which cables and pipes etc. are laid
and are big enough to drive through connect all the halls
to the technical control centre

Energieanlagen für stetige Leistungsabgabe wie ein Blockheizkraftwerk oder Geothermie schieden prinzipiell aus. Flexiblere Brennwertkessel mit Gasbetrieb, auf Öl umschaltbar, erhielten den Vorzug. Installiert wurden drei Kessel mit zusammen 15,2 Megawatt Leistung sowie Kältemaschinen mit umweltfreundlicher Ammoniaktechnik und ein 800 Kubikmeter fassender Eisspeicher, der die Beschränkung der Kälteproduktion auf die günstigere Nachtstromzeit erlaubt.

Doch Wärme und Kälte müssen in die riesigen Hallen gebracht werden. Dies geschieht üblicherweise durch konditionierte Luft, die in die Hallen eingeblasen wird. Und dies geschieht ebenso üblicherweise durch Drallluftauslässe an der Decke, die von oben warme Luft in die Halle quirlen, wodurch eine ständige Mischung des gesamten Hallenvolumens erreicht wird. Eine andere Version ist, mittels »Weitwurfdüsen« von den Wänden aus Frischluft in die Räume zu pusten.

Frischluft scheibenweise

Bei der Landesmesse wurde eine bislang nur im Büro- und Industriebereich eingesetzte Alternative gewählt, die Schichtlüftung. Dabei fließt die konditionierte Frischluft wie eine Flüssigkeit aus vier großformatigen Öffnungen in die Halle und verteilt sich gleichmäßig zwischen den Messeständen. Die verbrauchte Luft wird an den Wänden auf halber Höhe abgesaugt. Voluminöse (und hässliche) Luftkanäle an den Decken entfallen.

Den theoretischen Planungen und Computersimulationen folgten Versuchsreihen im Maßstab 1:1, für die in einer Messehalle auf dem Killesberg reale Messesituationen aufgebaut wurden. Das Institut für Gebäudeenergetik der Universität Stuttgart untersuchte die Wirksamkeit der Schichtlüftung im Testbetrieb und konnte nachweisen, dass auch 70 Meter breite Hallen ohne unbehagliche Zugerscheinungen belüftet werden können. Der entscheidende Vorteil ist der geringe Luftdurchsatz, denn es muss nicht die Halle in ihrer vollen Höhe und der gesamte Luftraum umgewälzt und konditioniert werden. Die Ersparnis gegenüber konventionellen Lüftungskonzepten beträgt auf alle Messehallen gerechnet

few of the 80 to 120 day trade fair days are very cold or very hot. The congress centre is also used for a maximum of 180 days a year, and capacity is rarely utilized to the full. The challenge was therefore to be able to cover peak loads at short notice, a requirement that does not necessarily inculcate huge enthusiasm among the in-house technicians.

Energy installations which can provide a constant energy output like a block-type thermal power station or geothermy were out of the question. Preference was given to more flexible condensing boilers which are based on gas but can be switched over to oil. Three boilers were installed with 15.2 megawatts of power combined. In addition, cooling machines based on environment-friendly ammonia technology as well as an 800 cubic metre cooling-capacity storage unit which enables cooling to be restricted to less expensive night-time electricity were used.

But hot and cold air has also to brought into the huge halls somehow. This is usually done by means of conditioned air blown into the halls and air outlets in the ceiling which force a whirling current of warm air into the hall below. This ensures that all the air in the hall is constantly mixed. Another method is to blow in fresh air from the walls with the help of wide-angle nozzles.

Fresh air in slices

For the state trade fair centre, an alternative was finally selected which had previously only been used in offices and industrial buildings: layered ventilation. With this system, the conditioned fresh air flows out of four large openings and into the hall like a liquid and spreads out uniformly between the trade fair stands. The used air is vacuum-removed half way up the walls. Large (and ugly) air ducts on the ceilings can thus be dispensed with.

The theoretical planning work and computer simulations were followed by a series of tests on a scale of 1:1, for which real trade fair situations were set up in a trade fair hall at the old Killesberg site. The Institut für Gebäudeenergetik (institute of building energy systems) of Stuttgart university investigated the effectiveness of layer ventilation in test mode and was able to verify that even 70 metre-wide halls can be ventilated without any uncomfortable draughts. The crucial advantage is

Lufttemperatur und Luftausbreitung
des Prinzips Schichtlüftung

Air temperature and air dispersion
during layered ventilation

01 Lufttemperatur in °C / Air temperature in °C
02 Lufttemperatur in °C in 1 m Höhe /
    Air temperature in °C at a height of 1 m
03 in 2 m Höhe / At a height of 2 m
04 in 6 m Höhe / At a height of 6 m

Luftausbreitung:
Isoflächen des mittleren Luftalters

Air dispersion:
iso-surfaces of the average air age

01 nach 2 Minuten / After 2 minutes
02 nach 4 Minuten / After 4 minutes
03 nach 6 Minuten / After 6 minutes
04 nach 8 Minuten / After 8 minutes
05 nach 10 Minuten / After 10 minutes
06 nach 12 Minuten / After 12 minutes

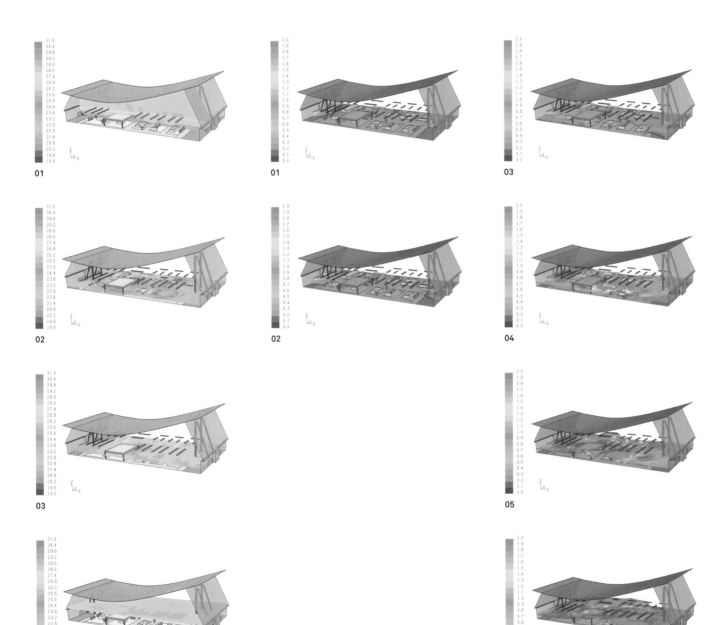

01

01

03

02

02

04

03

05

04

06

immerhin eine Million Kubikmeter Zuluft pro Stunde bzw. 30 Prozent, was sich nicht nur auf die Betriebskosten auswirkt, sondern auch schon beim Bau zu geringeren Dimensionierungen und damit Investitionen führt. Hinzu kommt die günstige Lage der Auslassöffnungen unmittelbar über den Leitungskanälen. Im Zusammenspiel mit der zentralen Heizungs- und Kältezentrale, die durch den Einfluss von DS-Plan von der Peripherie in die Nähe der Verbraucher im Untergeschoss des Congresscenters gerückt wurde, ergeben sich extrem kurze Leitungswege. Die Optimierung und die hohen Ablufttemperaturen ermöglichen zudem die ansonsten in Messehallen unwirtschaftliche Wärmerückgewinnung mit einem Rückwärmverhältnis von über 80 Prozent. Insgesamt ist die installierte Heizleistung mit 15,2 MW etwa im Vergleich zur neuen Messe in München flächenbezogen um ein Drittel geringer, die installierte Kälteleistung von 12,6 MW erreicht sogar nur knapp die Hälfte der Münchner Werte.

Allein 15 Millionen Euro an Investitionskosten sind durch die Optimierung eingespart worden. Mit diesem Lüftungskonzept und dem ebenfalls energiesparenden Einsatz eines hohen Anteils an Tageslicht, etwa in den Umbaupausen, profitiert die Landesmesse Stuttgart von entscheidenden Betriebskostenvorteilen im Energiesektor. Jährlich 275 MWh Solarstrom aus der auf den Dächern montierten Fotovoltaik fließen ebenfalls in das Energiesystem und bringen weitere Pluspunkte in der Ökobilanz. Die beispielhaften ökologischen Kennwerte der neuen Landesmesse sind nicht nur auf zeitgemäße Weise imagefördernd, sondern werden helfen, die Messe auch wirtschaftlich konkurrenzfähig zu halten.

the low air-flow rate as all the air right up to the roof of the hall does not have to be circulated and conditioned. The savings compared to conventional ventilation methods amounts to one million cubic metres of air per hour or 30 per cent for all the halls together. This not only has an effect on the operating costs but also requires less construction work and therefore a lower investment as well. Another benefit is the favourable position of the air outlets directly above the ducts. In conjunction with the heating and cooling control centre which was moved from the periphery to somewhere closer to the loads in the basement of the congress centre as a result of arguments presented by DS-Plan, the pipe conduits are therefore extremely short. Moreover, optimisation and the high temperatures of the used air enable heat recovery at a rate of 80 per cent. Normally in trade fair halls, regaining heat in this way is not economically efficient. Altogether, the installed heating capacity of 15.2 MW compared to the new trade fair centre in Munich, for example, is a third less in respect of the areas involved, while the installed cooling capacity of 12.6 MW is less than half that of the Munich values.

A total of 15 million euros in investment costs was saved solely as a result of optimisation. With this ventilation concept and the energy-saving use of daylight instead of artificial light for much of the time, especially between fairs, the Stuttgart Trade Fair Centre profits from decisive benefits derived from the effects energy saving has on the operating costs. Every year, 275 MWh of solar power from the photovoltaic systems installed on the roofs also flows into the energy system and represents a further ecological improvement. The exemplary key ecological data of the new trade fair centre not only enhance its contemporary image but will also help to keep it competitive in terms of economic efficiency.

Beim Wiesenknopf-Ameisenbläuling zu Haus

Der Natur- und
Landschaftsschutz und
die Grünplanung
spielten beim Messebau
eine Hauptrolle

Where the Dusky Large Blue is at home

Nature and landscape
conservation and landscape
planning play a major
role in the construction of
trade fair centres

Beim Wiesenknopf-Ameisenbläuling zu Haus
Der Natur- und Landschaftsschutz und die Grünplanung spielten beim Messebau eine Hauptrolle

Wie lockt man Rebhuhnhähnchen mit dem Tonband? Wie zählt man Laufkäfer? Wo wächst der Mauerpfeffer? Solche Fragen beantwortet Dr. Friederike Hübner von der AG.L.N. Landschaftsplanung und Naturschutzmanagement, die mit dem Fachbeitrag Tiere und Pflanzen und dem landschaftspflegerischen Begleitplan beauftragt war. Kaum eine Baumaßnahme im Land wurde von den Naturschützern in den Reihen der Messegegner so argwöhnisch beäugt wie der Bau der Landesmesse und so kommt es, dass das Gelände wohl eine der bestuntersuchten Flächen außerhalb der Naturschutzgebiete ist. Die Bestandsaufnahme von Flora und Fauna als Grundlage für die gesetzlich vorgeschriebene spätere »Eingriffsausgleichsbilanzierung« umfasste 230 Hektar Filderareal, wovon die Baumaßnahme nur 89 Hektar in Anspruch nimmt. Keine Pflanzenart entging den Biologen, kein Laufkäfer entkam unerkannt. Ab 3 Uhr morgens waren die Ornithologen unterwegs, um die Vögel anhand ihres Gesangs zu erkennen und zu kartieren, um Brutansatz und Bruterfolg zu prüfen. Vier Rebhuhnpaare sind dort heimisch, haben sie festgestellt, und unter den zahlreichen Tagfaltern findet sich auch der seltene Dunkle Wiesenknopf-Ameisenbläuling (Maculinea nausithous), der sich den Luxus erlaubt, die Kombination einer einzigen Pflanzenart (Großer Wiesenknopf) und das Nest einer einzigen Knotenameisenart (Myrmica rubra) als Lebensraum zu suchen und alles andere zu verschmähen.

Where the Dusky Large Blue is at home
Nature and landscape conservation and landscape planning play a major role in the construction of trade fair centres

How do you attract a male partridge with a tape recorder? How do you count beetles? Where does the common stone crop grow? Such questions are answered by Dr. Friederike Hübner from AG.L.N. Landschaftsplanung und Naturschutzmanagement, which was engaged to examine flora and fauna issues and draw up a plan for landscape maintenance. Hardly any other construction project in the country was eyed with as much suspicion by conservationists as displayed by those who were opposed to the new state trade fair centre. This is probably why the site is one of the most investigated parcels of land outside natural conservation areas. The inventory of flora and fauna as the basis for the later, legally prescribed »ecological compensation« covered 230 hectares of land in the Filder area, only 89 hectares of which was used for building. The biologists did not overlook any species of plants or a single beetle. The ornithologists were up and about at 3.00 o'clock in the morning, listening for and mapping birds and their songs and checking breeding patterns and their success. They found that it was the habitat for four pairs of partridges and many varieties of butterfly, including the rare Dusky Large Blue (maculinea nausithous), who allows itself the luxury of choosing the combination of a single type of plant (burnet) and the nest of a single mymicine ant species (myrmica rubra = red ant) as its habitat.

Bestand Tiere und Pflanzen

Flora und Vegetation

- ☐ Naturdenkmal
- ☐ Biotope § 24a NatSchG inkl. Nummer

- ⟋⟋ Grenze Naturschutzgebiet
- ⟋⟋ Grenze Landschaftsschutzgebiet
- 🌳 Einzelbäume und Alleen

Allgemeines

- ⋯ Planfeststellungsgrenzen
- --- Grenze Untersuchungsgebiet
- Kataster

Fauna

- R Käferfallenstandorte mit Bezeichnung
- ⊙ Handaufsammlungen Laufkäfer

Tagfalter Gefährdete Arten

- 🦋 Maculinea nausithous
  RL BW 2; FFH-Art

Biotoptypen und Biotopnummern

- Gehölzfläche
- 9 Gartenland
- 1 Getreide (artenarm)
- 2 Getreide (mäßig artenreich)
- 3 Kartoffel
- 5 Mais (mäßig artenreich)
- 4 Mais (artenarm)
- 6 Rübenacker
- 7 Sonderkulturen
- 17 Ackerbrachen
- 17 Klee/Luzerne-Ansaat
- 17 Grünland (Weidelgras-Ansaat)
- 17 Grünlandansaat
- 17 Intensivgrünland
- 18 Obstwiese

- 17 Grasflur ruderal
- 19 Ruderalflur
- 15 Langwiesener See
- 14 Grabensohle wasserführend
- 12 Grabenrand Gras-dominiert
- 14 Grabensohle trocken
- 12 Staudenreiche, hygrophile Grabenränder und -säume
- 16 Binsenfluren
- 16 Röhricht
- 21 Flughafen
- 21 Siedlungsfläche
- Straßen
- 20 Straßenbegleitflächen
- Wege befestigt
- 8 Wege unbefestigt

Brutvögel und Nahrungsgäste
Wertgebende Arten

- Braunkehlchen
- Feldlerche
- Graureiher
- Hänfling
- Kiebitz
- Rebhuhn
- Rohrammer
- Schafstelze
- Schleiereule
- Steinschmätzer

- Sumpfrohrsänger
- Wiesenpieper
- Baumfalke
- Gebirgsstelze
- Sperber
- Blesshuhn
- Feldsperling
- Teichhuhn
- Teichrohrsänger
- Wachtel

0   600 m

So kam es zu Bewertungen der Ackerflächen, Wege und Wasserläufe nach Naturschutzkriterien in fünf Wertstufen. Ziel war, die vorhandenen Lebensräume für Flora und Fauna zu erhalten beziehungsweise verlorene im Rahmen von Ausgleichsmaßnahmen an anderer Stelle durch Aufwertung der dortigen Flächen zu ersetzen. Die Messegesellschaft hatte deshalb Äcker in der Umgebung erworben, die nun gezielt als Buntbrachen mit unterschiedlichem Bewuchs und seitlichen, nur gering bewachsenen Schwarzbrachen vorgehalten werden, um Vögeln und anderen Feldbewohnern die nötigen Rückzugsflächen zu bieten. 11,5 Hektar solcher Ausgleichsflächen finden sich eingestreut zwischen den normal bewirtschafteten Feldern im Umkreis der Messe, wodurch die Bewertung des Gesamtareals deutlich erhöht werden konnte. Zusätzliche Ersatzmaßnahmen wurden entfernter gelegen bei der Renaturierung der Körschmündung durchgeführt.

Auf der Vorarbeit der Landschaftspfleger konnten die Garten- und Landschaftsplaner Adler + Olesch aufbauen, die schon am Wettbewerb beteiligt waren und die alle Freiflächen innerhalb des Messegeländes zu gestalten hatten. Sie definierten drei Welten: die funktionale Welt (mit absolutem Vorrang), die vom Versorgungsverkehr bestimmt ist und den LKW-Pool, Ausstellerparkplätze und Anlieferhöfe beinhaltet, dann die Piazza, ein konvex gewölbter Vorplatz, der mit seinen Längen- und Breitengraden ein Stück Globus abbildet, sowie den Messepark in der Mittelachse der Anlage.

Immergrün und Hungerkünstler

Als Erholungsfläche zwischen den Hallen ist der Messepark ein intensiv genutzter Garten, den die Landschaftsarchitekten als Kontrast zur rationalen Architektur spielerisch gestalteten, mit geschwungenem Weg, modulierten Rasenflächen und frei interpretierter heimischer Vegetation, mit Buchen, Kiefern, Ahorn und immergrünen Hecken, die auch in der winterlichen Messesaison Wirkung zeigen.

In this way, the farmland, pathways and waterways were evaluated in five stages according to criteria of nature conservation. The aim was to retain existing habitats of flora and fauna and to replace lost ones elsewhere through a procedure of upgrading. The company which runs the trade fair centre had purchased farmland in the surrounding area for this reason. It was then kept as wildflower strips and fallow land at the sides with only a small amount of vegetation in order to provide birds and other field creatures with the necessary refuge. 11.5 hectares of such compensation land is scattered about between the normally farmed fields surrounding the trade fair centre, as a result of which the value of the site as a whole was considerably increased. Additional replacement measures were carried out a little further away where the place at which the river Körsch joins the river Neckar was restored to its natural state.

Landscape gardeners and planners Adler + Olesch, who had taken part in the competition and had to design all the open areas within the boundaries of the trade fair site, were able to build on the work done previously by the landscape conservationists. They defined three different »worlds«: the functional world (with absolute precedence) which is determined by traffic needs and includes the truck pool, exhibitors parking spaces and delivery yards, then the piazza, a convex-shaped forecourt shaped like part of a globe, and finally the trade fair park on the central axis.

Hardy plants and evergreens

As a recreational area between the halls, there is the trade fair park, an intensively used garden space which the landscape architects designed for pure pleasure in contrast to the rational architecture, featuring a curved path, modulated lawns and freely interpreted local vegetation, with beech, fir and maple trees and evergreen hedges which serve their purpose even during the winter season.

Bewertung Tiere und Pflanzen

Allgemeines

0   600 m

Katasterdaten
Untersuchungsgebietsgrenze

Wertstufen

1   sehr gering
2   gering
2,5 gering bis mittel (nur Laufkäfer)
3   mittel
4   hoch
5   sehr hoch (nicht vergeben)

Bewertung Flora und Vegetation (Pflanzen)

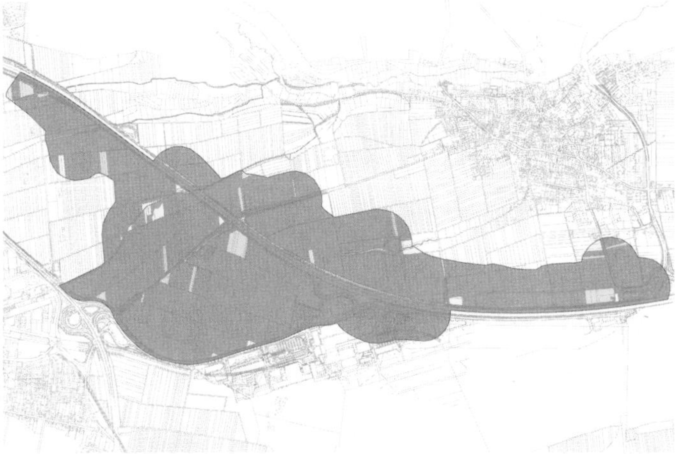

Bewertung Tagfalter

Bewertung Avifauna (Vögel)

Bewertung Laufkäfer

Die Grünflächen um die Hallen ordnen sich eher dem architektonisch strengen Lageplan unter. LKW-Pool und Stellplätze sind als Schotterrasenflächen angelegt, um die großflächige Versiegelung zu vermeiden. In Stauraumkanälen und Retentionsterrassen wird das Regenwasser gestaut und gereinigt, bis es der Kapazität des Lachengrabens entsprechend mit 20 Liter pro Sekunde langsam abfließt. Denn der Regenwasserhaushalt gehört ebenfalls zu den Obliegenheiten der Landschaftsplaner.

Die Umgehungsstraße und die Heerstraße werden von Alleebäumen – Ahorn, Spitzahorn, Esche – begleitet, in den Höfen stehen Platanen. Auch die Begrünung der Hallendächer gilt als effektive Ausgleichsmaßnahme. 40.000 Kubikmeter Substrat aus Humus, Ton und Lava wurden auf die mit Vliesmatten vorbereiteten Dachflächen aufgebracht und mit einer speziellen Samenmischung dotiert. Es sind Sukkulenten, »Hungerkünstler«, die auf den Dächern gedeihen und dort Schmetterlingen, Insekten und Hautflüglern eine Heimat ohne Fressfeinde bieten.

Eine knifflige Aufgabe hatte die Flughafengesellschaft als Betreiber des Parkhauses den Gartenplanern gestellt: Die Brücken sollten allzeit grün sein, aber nicht ständig gemäht werden müssen. Ein Versuchsaufbau mit 24 Feldern und verschiedenen Beimischungen zum Filderlehm wurde von der Universität Hohenheim zwei Jahre lang gefahren, um die optimalen Verhältnisse für die Parkhausbegrünung zu ermitteln.

Ansonsten verlangten die Landschaftspfleger »autochtone Samenmischungen« zur Begrünung des Messegeländes einzusetzen, das heißt ortstypische Pflanzenfamilien, die für Flora und Fauna mit dem Filderraum harmonieren, immer mit dem Ziel, die Beeinträchtigung des Ökosystems durch den Messekomplex so gering wie möglich zu halten und der Natur möglichst zurückzugeben, was ihr genommen wurde.

The green areas around the halls tend to be dominated by the architecturally strict site plan. The truck pool and the parking spaces have crushed stone surfaces, used to avoid a sealed covering over the ground. Rainwater is collected and cleaned in channels and retention terraces before flowing slowly away at 20 litres per second. After all, rainwater management was also one of the responsibilities of the landscape gardeners.

The bypass road and Heerstrasse have maple, oak and ash trees along them and, in the courtyards, there are plane trees. The landscaping of the hall roofs is also an effective part of ecological compensation. 40,000 cubic metres of substrate, composed of humus, clay and lava was placed on the roofs, which had been prepared with fleece mats. This substrate was then planted with a special mixture of seeds. They produce dense growth which flourishes on the roofs and provides a home for butterflies, insects and moths without any predators.

As the operator of the multi-storey car park, the airport company had given the garden planners a tricky task: the bridges were to be green at all times without having to be continually mowed. A test with 24 plots and different mixtures added to the Filder clay was conducted by the university of Hohenheim over a period of two years in order to find out the best ratios for planting the multi-storey car park.

Apart from this, the landscape conservationists demanded »autochtone seed mixtures« for landscaping the trade fair site. These are plant families which are typical of the location and harmonize with the flora and fauna of the Filder area. The aim is to minimize the burden placed on the ecosystem by the trade fair complex and to give as much back to nature as was taken from it by the site.

Vermeidung und Minderung von Eingriffen

✳ M13: Ökologische Baubegleitung: Ausweisung sensibler Bereiche in den Flächen bauzeitlicher Inanspruchnahme

Rekultivierungsflächen

Ⓐ M8: Brache
Ⓑ A7: Acker
Ⓒ M8: Grünland
Ⓓ M8: Grünland
Ⓔ A7: Extensive Gras- und Krautflur

Grundlagen

···· Planfeststellungsgrenze
Projekt S 21
— Katasterdaten

Flächenbelegungen bei Gebäude und Wegenetz

Straßenbankett
Straßenmulde
Versiegelte Flächen
Wirtschaftsweg unbefestigt
Wirtschaftsweg wassergebundene Decke
Fuß- und Radweg befestigt

Maßnahmenflächen »Retentionsbecken«

M15 + M16: Standortsgerechte Laubbäume
M15 + M16: Retentionsbecken und Grabenböschung
M15 + M16: Retentionsbeckenmulden und -graben
M15 + M16: Standortsgerechte Laubbäume (Weidenfaschinen)
☆ M11: Einzelbaumschutz
M10: Schutz von Maculinea nausithous

Kompensationsmaßnahmen im Messeumfeld

M3: Kies- und Schotterflächen
M3: Rasengitter
M1 + M2: Extensive Dachbegrünung (teils mit Gehölzpflanzungen)
M7: Extensive Glatthaferwiese
M3 + M9: Alleen und Parkplatzbäume (Landschaftliche Einbindung)
M4 – M6: Gestalterisch wirkende Bäume
M5: Messesee
M5: Grünfläche
M5: Zierhecken

M14: Wiederherstellung Rennenbach

Krautreiche Grabenböschungen
Wasserführende Sohle

Maßnahmenflächen »Feldbewohnende Fauna«

Übergeordnet wirken hier A9 + A10

A1: Buntbrache
A1 + A2: Schwarzbrache
A2: Fabaceen- / Ölfruchteinsaat
A3: Niedrige Feldhecke
A4: Altgrasstreifen
A5: Erdweg freihalten

Rekultivierung bauzeitlich in Anspruch genommener Flächen

M11 + M12: Acker
M11 + M1: Grünland
M11 – M14: wie vorherige bzw. angrenzende Nutzung
A6: Obstbaum / -wiese

Kompensationsmaßnahmen der Straßennebenflächen

M9: Gehölzpflanzungen
A8: Verpflanzung von nach § 32 NatSchG geschützten Hecken
M9: Extensive Gras- und Krautfluren
M9: Laubbäume auf Straßennebenflächen
M9: Alleen

0   400 m

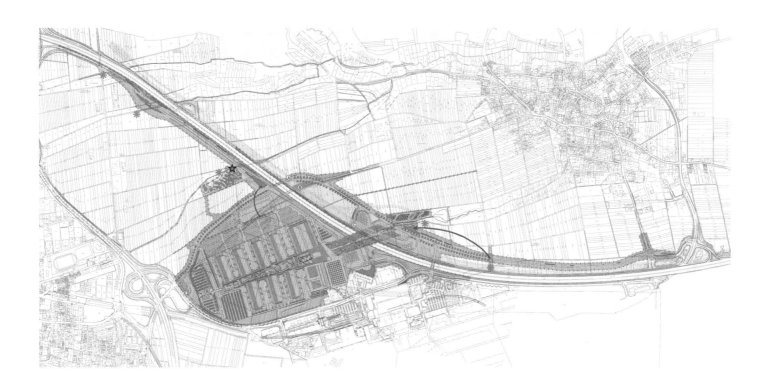

alle 3
all

↑ Ausg
Exit

alle 6
all

← 🍽

ongress
ongress

↑ Mess
Fairc

alle 1
all

↑ Freig
Outd

Woher? Wohin?
Die »Farben der Nationen«
des Informations- und
Orientierungssystems führen
auf den rechten Weg

Where from? Where to?
The »colours of the nations«
of the information
and signage system point
the way

Woher? Wohin?
Die »Farben der Nationen«
des Informations- und
Orientierungssystems führen
auf den rechten Weg

Welche Farben hat die Welt der Messe? Aus welcher Höhe beobachtet ein LKW-Fahrer die Situation vor seiner Windschutzscheibe? Wie lassen sich Hinweise in verschiedenen Sprachen trennen? Darf ein Brezel-Piktogramm grün sein? Tausend Fragen auch dieser Art sind zu beantworten, bis eine Messe funktioniert. Ein grafisches Informations- und Orientierungssystem ist unverzichtbar, denn kaum jemand wird sich auf einem Riesenareal dieses Zuschnitts ohne Orientierungshilfen zurechtfinden, nicht die Anlieferer, nicht die Aussteller, nicht die Messebesucher und nicht die Kongressgäste. Die allgegenwärtige, eine mehrstufige Hierarchie bildende Beschilderung bestimmt aber auch in besonderem Maß das Erscheinungsbild der Messe und ist deshalb als Marketingfaktor von Belang. So wird vom damit beauftragten Grafikdesigner nicht nur verlangt, dass er die Menschen möglichst unmerklich, jedenfalls möglichst irrtumsfrei über das Gelände führt, sondern dass er gleichzeitig der Messe auch ein unverwechselbares, positiv gestimmtes Bild verleiht. Die Messe als eine Marke ist das Ziel, die im harten Wettstreit der Messestandorte Vorteile verschaffen soll.

Der Stuttgarter Kommunikationsdesigner Andreas Uebele, Projektleiterin Katrin Dittman und ihr Team konnten mit ihren Vorschlägen und den »Farben der Nationen« überzeugen. Ohne Scheu vor Buntheit orientierten sie sich an den Flaggen aller Nationen und bemühten die ganze Palette der zur Verfügung stehenden Farben. Lediglich Braun mochten sie nicht einsetzen und das ist wohl auch auf keiner Nationalflagge zu finden, will man einmal von Katar absehen.

Bei diesem Ansatz ist freilich die Gefahr groß, ins beliebig Bunte abzugleiten. Deshalb wird das Prinzip der Leitfarben ins Spiel gebracht. Die Farben helfen bei der Orientierung, keine Farbe ist willkürlich und dekorativ eingesetzt, jede hat etwas zu bedeuten. So kommt Buntheit nur dort auf, wo verteilt wird, wo es beispielsweise nach links in die Halle 1 (Orangetöne), geradeaus zum Ausgang Ost (Blau) und nach rechts zum Congresscenter (Rottöne) und zum Freigelände (Grün) geht.

Where from? Where to?
The »colours of the nations«
of the information
and signage system point
the way

What are the colours of the trade fair centre? From what height does a truck driver see what is happening in front of him? How can instructions in different languages be separated? Is it o.k. for a pretzel pictogram to be green? There are thousands of such questions which have to be answered before a trade fair centre can function properly. A graphic information and signage system is indispensable in this context as hardly anyone would be able find their way about such a complex facility without some form of guidance – not the delivery drivers, not the exhibitors, not the visitors and not the congress guests. The ubiquitous signs conceived in the form of a multiple-level hierarchy exert a particularly strong influence on the appearance of the trade fair centre and are therefore also important as a marketing factor for the venue. It was therefore demanded from the graphic designer engaged for this purpose not only that people should be guided as imperceptibly and accurately as possible around the grounds but also that a memorable positive image was to be created at the same time. The trade fair centre as a brand was the objective of this requirement so that advantages would be generated in the tough competition between trade fair centres.

The Stuttgart communications designer, Andreas Uebele, project manager Katrin Dittman and her team presented convincing arguments with their proposals and their idea for »colours of the nations«. Unafraid of using a wide variety of colours to perform the required functions, they based their design on the flags of all nations and utilised the entire range of colours available. They only avoided brown, a colour which is found on no national flag, except for Qatar's.

Adopting such an approach, of course, involves the danger of a random confusion of too much colour and variation. The principle of colours for navigation was therefore applied. The colours assist orientation, are not used arbitrarily or for decoration, and each one has a particular meaning. A combination of many colours therefore only occurs in places where the flow of visitors divides, for example to the left into hall 1 (shades of orange), straight ahead to the east exit (blue), to the right towards the congress centre (shades of red) and to the area outside (green).

Seite 190
Die Farbpalette des Informations- und
Orientierungssystems der Messe
ist den Flaggen der Länder entlehnt

Page 190
The colour scheme of the information
and signage system of the trade fair centre
is based on national flags

01 Informations- und Orientierungssystem
mittels unterschiedlicher Kennfarben
für die geraden und die ungeraden Hallenreihen
und die verschiedenen Funktionen

Information and signage system,
using different identifying colours for the odd
and even series of halls and for a variety
of different functions

02 Kennfarben im Außenbereich

Identifying colours outdoors

03 Die Schrift Avenir, 1988 von Adrian Frutiger
entworfen. Soweit möglich, verweisen
international verständliche Piktogramme auf die
Funktionen. Richtungspfeile für alle Hinweise

›Avenir‹, designed by Adrian Frutiger in 1988.
Wherever possible, internationally comprehensible
pictograms explain the functions. Direction
arrows for all locations

01

Service	
S 0585 - Y30R	
S 0580 - Y20R	

Halle 1	
S 0585 - Y50R	
S 0585 - Y30R	

Hallen 3, 5, 7, 9	
S 0585 - Y80R	
S 0585 - Y60R	

Hallen 2, 4, 6, 8	
S 1070 - R10B	
S 1085 - Y90R	

Kongress	
S 1070 - R20B	
S 1060 - R30B	

VIP-Service	
S 3050 - R50B	
S 2050 - R50B	

02

Stelen	
S 1075 - G50Y	
S 1070 - G70Y	

Freigelände	
S 2075 - G20Y	
S 2070 - G30Y	

Schnittstellen	
S 3065 - R90B	
S 2065 - R90B	

03

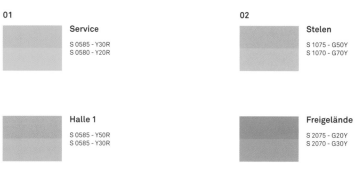

01 Stellung von Schrift und unterlegten
Farbstreifen zueinander

Relationship of writing and underlying
coloured strips to each other

02 Schriftgrößen, Schildgrößen und modulare
Entwicklung des Schildaufbaus

Writing sizes, sign sizes and modular
development of the sign structure

03 Systematische Vergrößerungsschritte
von Richtungspfeilen und Schrift

Systematic enlargement of direction
arrows and writing

04 Die Stelen sind aus dem Modulsystem der
Schilder entwickelt. In welcher Höhe die
Information angeboten wird, hängt von dem
Lesenden ab. Die Ausschnitte reagieren
auf die Größe der Stele.

The columns are created from the modular
system of the signs. The height at which
the information is displayed depends on the
legend while the cut-out sections are in
relation to the size of the columns.

01

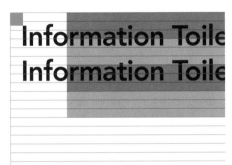

02

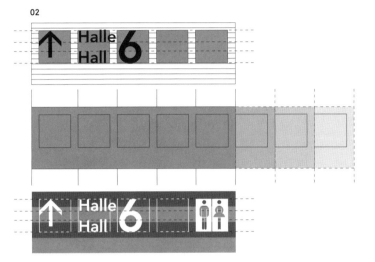

03

04

Das Farbsystem reicht von einem dunklen Gelb für Serviceeinrichtungen, Restaurants, Toiletten usw. über Orange für die Hallenspange mit den ungeraden Zahlen und Rot-Pink für die geraden Zahlen bis zum Congresscenter mit Magenta. Lila bedeutet VIP-Service, Grün verweist auf das Freigelände, während die große Gruppe der Hinweisschilder für Verkehr, Aus- und Eingänge und dergleichen durch blaue Töne codiert ist.

Manche Bedeutungen sind eingängig und werden spontan rezipiert, andere Zusammenhänge, beispielsweise die Unterschiede der Hallen mit geraden und ungeraden Zahlen, wird man intuitiv wahrnehmen. Es wird natürlich auch Zeitgenossen geben, die ganz genau hinsehen und sich darüber Gedanken machen. Die werden das System problemlos durchschauen und optimal davon profitieren können.

Wohlgelauntes Augenzwinkern

Nicht nach der reinen Lehre des legendären Designers Otl Aicher (Olympia 1972 in München), von dem die noch immer gültigen Piktogramme stammen, hat Uebele auch ein gestalterisch-ästhetisches Anliegen, das sich nicht aus der puren Funktionalität entwickeln lässt. Indem er die gewählten Ordnungsfarben jeweils in helleren und dunkleren Streifen auf die Schilder bringt, entsteht eine neue Qualität, ein Augenzwinkern, wird plötzlich eine bestimmte Atmosphäre vermittelt, eine wohlgelaunte Stimmung, die der Messe Stuttgart, und nur ihr, zu eigen ist.

Natürlich ist auch diese Idee nicht ungefährlich, könnte zur Verspieltheit und zum Selbstzweck tendieren. Deshalb wurden die Nuancen nicht zu kontrastreich gewählt. Sie gehen immer noch zusammen, bilden einen Farbteppich unter der Beschriftung. Und damit die Schrift auf dem Teppich bleibt und nicht mit den Streifen kollidiert, dürfen die Linien der Streifen nicht mit den Begrenzungslinien der Schrift zusammenfallen.

Als Schrift wurde die 1988 von Adrian Frutiger entwickelte Avenir Heavy ausgewählt, als Alternative, etwa für Türschilder, der Schnitt Avenir Roman. Die rundliche, perlige Schrift soll sich möglichst wenig mit dem untergelegten Streifenmuster verbinden.

The colour scheme ranges from dark yellow for service facilities, restaurants, toilets etc., to orange for the row of halls with uneven numbers, red-pink for the even numbers and magenta for the congress centre. Purple means VIP service, green is a pointer to the outside while the many direction signs for traffic, entrances, exits and the like are coded in shades of blue.

Many meanings are immediately apparent and are spontaneously understood while other interrelationships such as the differences between the halls with odd and even numbers are grasped intuitively. There will, of course, be some people who take a closer look and think deliberately about where they want to go. They will understand the system with ease and be able to use it to best purpose.

A friendly wink

Ignoring the undiluted theory of the legendary designer Otl Aicher (Olympia 1972 in Munich), from whom the still effective pictograms originate, Uebele pursues an aesthetics of design that is not derived from pure functionality. By applying the selected ordering colours in the form of light and dark stripes on the signs, he creates a new contextual quality, a wink of the eye at it were. Suddenly, a certain atmosphere is conveyed, an expansiveness of mood, which is particular to the Stuttgart Trade Fair Centre.

Of course, this idea is not without its hazards as it could tend towards playful idiosyncrasy and become an end in itself. The chosen nuances of colour do not excessively contrast with each other. They always go together, forming a tapestry of colours beneath the writing on the sign. To avoid collisions between the writing and the stripes, the lines of the stripes are not allowed to coincide with the limiting lines of the writing.

The font selected is Avenir Heavy developed by Adrian Frutiger in 1988 and, as an alternative for door signs for example, Avenir Roman was chosen. The round pearly font is intended to stand out from the underlying pattern of stripes.

Die Farben weisen den Weg: gelbe und rote zur
Messe, rosa zum Kongress, blaue zu den Ausgängen,
grüne zu den Freiflächen

The colours show the visitor where to go: yellow
and red to the trade fair centre, pink to the
congress hall, blue to the exits and green to the
outdoor areas

An den Wänden verbindet sich das
Informations- und Orientierungssystem
mit den Architekturfarben

On the walls, the information
and signage system is combined with
the colours of the architecture

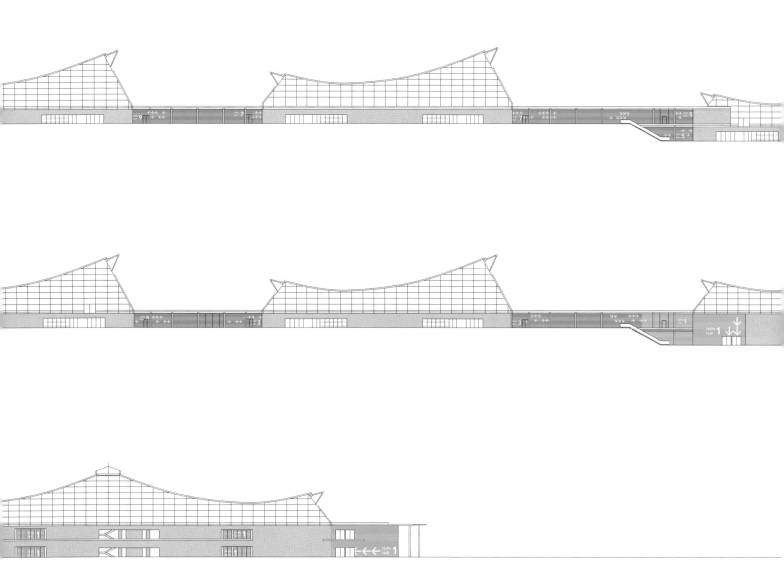

Stelen im Freibereich in ausreichender Größe
sind Wegweiser und Hinweise fürs Parken

Sufficiently large columns in the outdoor area serve
as signposts and display parking information

Ein genau definiertes Raster mit festgelegten Größenverhältnissen und Hierarchien ist Grundlage jeden Schildes und jeden Piktogramms. So ergeben sich Schriftgrade, Abstände, Ränder und dergleichen »von selbst« und jeder Typus eines Schildes hat seine zugewiesene Größe. Abweichungen können durch die Architektur gegeben sein: Ist die Hallenkennzeichnung auf der Giebelfront anzubringen, wird sich das Schild am Raster der Glasfassade ausrichten müssen. Gleiches gilt für die Betonwände zwischen den Hallen, die, mit großflächigen Farbfeldern versehen, zwar dem Farbleitsystem, nicht jedoch dem proportionalen Raster untergeordnet sein können. Auf Eingänge wird gleich mit einer ganzen Schar von Pfeilen hingewiesen. Mehr Richtungsvorgabe und mehr Aufforderungscharakter ist kaum möglich.

Selbstverständlich haben sich die Designer auch bemüht, für die Ladenschilder Prinzipien zu entwickeln. Die kommerziellen Nutzungen lassen sich jedoch erfahrungsgemäß gestalterisch kaum »domestizieren«. Außerdem hängt das Erscheinungsbild der Shops von der dauerhaft konsequenten Beachtung des Gestaltungskanons durch die Messegesellschaft ab.

Eine besondere Form gab das Team Uebele den Kommunikationsmitteln im Außenbereich und auf der Plaza. Dort stehen bis zu 8,5 Meter hohe »Stelenfahnen« mit einseitigem Fuß in der Messegrundfarbe Hellgelb für Hinweise und Messeplakate und kleinere in Grün oder Blau für Informationen und Parkhinweise.

Die beherzte Farbkomposition des Kommunikationssystems ist sicher ein Wagnis und ein Vabanquespiel zwischen ästhetischem Ausdruck und nüchterner Funktion. Doch wenn das Wagnis gelingen sollte, was sich mit der Zeit im Messebetrieb erweisen wird, ist es zweifellos ein Gewinn für die Neue Messe Stuttgart, ein atmosphärischer für die Messebesucher und ein Imagegewinn für die Messe als Marke.

An exactly defined pattern with specified sizes and hierarchies is the basis of each sign and pictogram. This »automatically« determines the font size, spaces, edges and the like and each type of sign has its own assigned size. Deviations may be dictated by the architecture. For example, if the hall number is to be fitted to the gable front, the sign has to align itself to the grid pattern of the glass facade. The same applies to the concrete walls between the halls. They have large patches of colour and can be subordinated to the colour guidance system but not to the proportional grid pattern. An abundance of arrows point to entrances. A larger number of directional indications and instructional pointers would hardly be conceivable.

Of course, the designers also tried to develop a set of principles for the shop signs. However, experience has shown that commercial uses are very difficult to »domesticate« in respect of their design. Apart from this, the appearance of the shop depends on sustained and consistent compliance with the design canon by the company responsible for operating the trade fair centre.

For the means of communication outside and in the piazza, the Uebele team devised a special system. Here, there are »flags« up to 8.5 metres high with a leg on one side in the basic colour of the trade fair centre, namely bright yellow, for signs and trade fair posters. There are also smaller ones in green or blue for information and parking.

The animated colour range for the communication system is no doubt a risky choice and a Vabanque game between aesthetic expression and sober functionality. But if the choice is successful – something that only time will tell – it will without doubt be a gain for the new Stuttgart Trade Fair Centre, an atmospheric benefit for its visitors and an image boost for the new trade fair centre as a brand in its own right.

Zeittafel

07.12.1993
Veröffentlichung des
Standortgutachtens
Messe 2000 mit
der Empfehlung
»Echterdinger Ei-Ost«

18.03.1994
Bund und Land beschließen
den Bau eines ICE-Bahnhofs
Flughafen

12.10.1995
Beschluss des Gemeinderats
Stuttgart zugunsten der
Messe außerhalb der Markung

18.03.1997
Land, Region und Stadt
beschließen das
Finanzierungskonzept

14.05.1998
Gründung der Projektgesellschaft
Neue Messe GmbH & Co. KG
durch die Gesellschafter Land Baden-
Württemberg (45 %) und
Landeshauptstadt Stuttgart (45 %)
sowie Verband Region Stuttgart (10 %)

23.09.1998
Ulrich Bauer zum Geschäftsführer
der Projektgesellschaft Neue Messe
GmbH & Co. KG bestellt

10.12.1998
Verabschiedung des
Landesmessegesetzes
durch den Landtag

12.02.1999
Vorstellung des
Testentwurfs

30.03.1999
Auslobung des europaweiten
Architektenwettbewerbs
1. Phase

08.06.1999
Juryentscheidung 1. Phase,
Auswahl von 30 Entwürfen für
die 2. Phase

06.07.1999
Architektenwettbewerb
2. Phase

05.11.1999
Teiländerung des Regionalplans
mit Ausweisung des
Messestandorts tritt in Kraft

10.11.1999
Juryentscheidung 2. Phase,
Auswahl drei 1. Preise,
Einstieg in die Optimierungsphase

11.02.2000
Juryentscheidung Optimierungs-
phase zugunsten des Entwurfs
Wulf & Partner

26.06.2001
Antrag der Projektgesellschaft
auf Planfeststellung beim
Regierungspräsidium Stuttgart

08.07.2002
Finanzierungsvereinbarung der
Gesellschafter

12.03.2003
Planfeststellungsbeschluss
durch das Regierungspräsidium

15.05.2003
letztinstanzliches Urteil
des Bundesverwaltungsgerichts
zugunsten der Messe

14.09.2004
1. Spatenstich

15.06.2005
Grundsteinlegung

27.09.2006
Richtfest

06.02.2007
alle Klagen gegen den
Planfeststellungsbeschluss
rechtskräftig abgewiesen

13.06.2007
erste Messe
Blechexpo/Schweisstec 2007
in den Hallen 3–8

19.10.2007
Einweihung

Chronology

07.12.1993
Trade fair location study 2000
with the recommendation
»Echterdinger Ei-Ost« (egg-shaped
piece of land in east Echterdingen)

18.03.1994
Federal government and the
state decide on an ICE railway station
for the airport

12.10.1995
Decision of Stuttgart council in
favour of a trade fair centre outside
the city limits

18.03.1997
The state, region and city adopt
the financing concept

14.05.1998
Establishment of the project
company Neue Messe GmbH & Co. KG
by the State of Baden-Württemberg
(45 %), the state capital Stuttgart
(45 %) and Verband Region Stuttgart
(10 %) acting as partners

23.09.1998
Ulrich Bauer appointed managing
director of the project company
Neue Messe GmbH & Co. KG

10.12.1998
Ratification of the state trade fair law
by the Landtag (state parliament)

12.02.1999
Presentation of the test design

30.03.1999
Issue of invitation to take part in
the Europe-wide architectural competition, 1st phase

08.06.1999
Jury verdict in 1st phase, selection of
30 designs for the 2nd phase

06.07.1999
2nd phase of architectural
competition

05.11.1999
Partial change in the regional plan
with indication of the trade fair
centre's location comes into force

10.11.1999
Jury verdict in 2nd phase, selection
of three 1st prize winners

11.02.2000
Jury verdict for refinement phase,
design of Wulf & Partner

26.06.2001
Application of the project company
for planning approval submitted
to the Stuttgart regional council

08.07.2002
Financing agreement of the partners

12.03.2003
Planning approval by the government
presidium

15.05.2003
Final verdict of the Federal
Administrative Court in favour of the
trade fair center

14.09.2004
1st cut of the spade

15.06.2005
Foundation stone laid

27.09.2006
Topping out ceremony

06.02.2007
All actions against the planning
approval decision legally dismissed

13.06.2007
First trade fair:
Blechexpo/Schweisstec 2007
in halls 3–8

19.10.2007
Inauguration

Technische Daten

Standort
Landesmesse Stuttgart GmbH
Messepiazza
70629 Stuttgart

Investitionskosten
806 Millionen Euro einschließlich
Baunebenkosten, Grundstück,
Außenanlagen und Ausstattung

Kernmessefläche
60 ha

Äußere Verkehrserschließung
23 ha

Ausgleichsflächen Renaturierung
11 ha

Bruttogrundfläche
432.000 m²

Bruttorauminhalt
3.000.000 m³

Ausstellungsfläche
103.300 m²

Ausstellung Freigelände
40.000 m² Schotterrasenfläche

Parkplätze gedeckt
4900

Parkplätze offen
1800

Grünflächen Umfeld
36.000 m²

Messepark
21.000 m² Belag,
11.000 m² Rasen
Bäume 541
Alleebäume Landstraße L 1192
188

Dachbegrünung Parkhaus
21.000 m²

Dachbegrünung Hallen
33.300 m²

Bewegte Erdmassen
1,8 Millionen m³

Tragwerkstahl
50.000 t

Bewehrungsstahl
15.000 t

Beton
600.000 m³

Stromanschlussleistung
23 MW

Wärmeerzeugungsleistung
15,2 MW

Kälteerzeugungsleistung
12,6 MW

Fotovoltaik Jahresertrag
275 MWh

Hochhalle
25.000 m² Ausstellungsfläche,
lichte Höhe 14 m,
4560 m² Nebennutzung,
7580 m² Technik,
Bodenbelastbarkeit 50 kN/m²,
Galerie 10 kN/m²,
Elektroversorgung 100 W/m²,
Beleuchtung 300 Lux

7 Standardhallen
je 10.500 m²
Ausstellungsfläche,
lichte Höhe 10 m
Bodenbelastbarkeit
Bodenplatte 50 kN/m²,
Elektroversorgung 100 W/m²,
Beleuchtung 300 Lux

**ICS Internationales
Congresscenter Stuttgart**
Halle 4800 m²,
lichte Höhe 11 m
Saal 2900 m²,
2300 Plätze
9 Seminarräume mit
insgesamt 690 Plätzen
8 Mietbüros mit
insgesamt 220 m²

Gastronomie
2 Hauptrestaurants mit
insgesamt 640 Plätzen
11 Bistros/Bars je 30–35 Plätze
Vita-Café 35 Plätze

Läden
Messeshop, Backshop,
insgesamt 190 m²

Technical data

Address
Landesmesse Stuttgart GmbH
Messepiazza
70629 Stuttgart

Investment costs
Euro 806 million, including
auxiliary construction
costs, land, outdoor
installations and equipment

Core trade fair area
60 ha

Outside area for traffic access
23 ha

**Compensation areas
for restoration to nature**
11 ha

Gross ground area
432,000 m²

Gross volume of space
3,000,000 m³

Exhibition floor space
103,300 m²

Outdoor exhibition area
40,000 m² of
ballast covered with grass

Parking spaces, covered
4900

Parking spaces, open-air
1800

Surrounding landscaped area
36,000 m²

Trade fair park
21,000 m² with hard surface,
11,000 m² with grass
Trees 541
Avenue trees, highway L 1192
188

**Green area on top of
multi-storey car park**
21,000 m²

Green areas on top of halls
33,300 m²

Amount of earth moved
1.8 million m³

Steel for load-bearing structure
50,000 t

Reinforcing steel
15,000 t

Concrete
600,000 m³

Electric power supply
23 MW

Heat generating capacity
15.2 MW

Cold generating capacity
12.6 MW

**Annual energy yield
of photovoltaic systems**
275 MWh

High hall
25,000 m² of exhibition floor space,
clear height 14 m,
4560 m² for auxiliary uses,
7580 m² for technical systems,
load-bearing capacity
of floor 50 kN/m²,
gallery 10 kN/m²,
electrical supply 100 W/m²,
lighting 300 lux

7 standard halls
Each with 10,500 m² of
exhibition floor space,
clear height 10 m,
load-bearing capacity of
floor slab 50 kN/m²,
electrical supply 100 W/m²,
lighting 300 lux

**ICS International
Congress Center Stuttgart**
Hall: 4800 m²,
clear height 11 m
Conference room:
2900 m², 2300 seats
9 seminar rooms
with a total of 690 seats
8 offices for rent
with a total floor space
of 220 m²

Catering
2 main restaurants with a
total of 640 seats
11 bistros/bars
each with 30–35 seats
Vita Café with 35 seats

Shops
Trade fair shop, bakery,
total 190 m²

Projektbeteiligte
Project participants

Bauherr
Projektgesellschaft Neue Messe
GmbH & Co. KG, Stuttgart

Geschäftsführer
Ulrich Bauer
Ulrich Kromer von Baerle
Walter Schoefer

Prokuristen
Wolfgang Maier
Hans-Ulrich Rollmann

Mitarbeiter
Helmut Ebinger
Thomas Glawa
Eberhard Gessert
Elvine-Isabella Schuller
Christian Witt
Michaela Reiter

Berater
Albert Ackermann
Martin Schlenker

Nutzer
Landesmesse
Stuttgart GmbH, Stuttgart
Geschäftsführer
Ulrich Kromer von Baerle

Architekten
Wulf & Partner, Stuttgart
Tobias Wulf, Kai Bierich,
Alexander Vohl

Mitarbeiter
Matteo Ammirati
Harald Baumann
Björn Berg
Beate von Bischopinck
Andrea Block-Roß
Regina Brenner
Christina Bröckel
Nils Buchmann
Jo Carle
    (Oberbauleiter)
Cordula Currle
Alexander Dambacher
Joe Deutinger
Andreas Ditschuneit
Alexander Domme
Daniela Dreher
Izabella Hajkowska
Anke Hentze
Camilo Hernandez
Indre Herrmann
Stefan Hoppe
Carsten Koglin
Stephan Kolmer
Waldemar Kolotzek
Albrecht Krepp
Jonas Lechler

Axel Mannhorst
Martin Meixner
Ingmar Menzer
Andreas Moll
Lars Neininger
Volker Prokoph
Daniel Raiser
Zeki Samer
Christian Schlameuß
Sonja Schmuker
Andreas Schneider
Stefan Schönstein
Thomas Schulz
Sebastian Stocker
Gaston Stoff
Jochen Stopper
Cordula Volk
Kristina Volland
Steffen Vogt
    (Projektleitung gesamt)
Sandra Wenzler
Maja Zeppernick
Andreas Zürcher
Achim Zumpfe

Landschaftsarchitekten
Adler & Olesch, Nürnberg
Michael Adler, Ralf Strasser

Projektsteuerung Messe
Drees & Sommer Stuttgart GmbH,
Projektmanagement und
bautechnische Beratung, Stuttgart
Geschäftsführer Thomas Jaißle

**Projektsteuerung äußere
Verkehrserschließung**
Drees & Sommer Infra, Consult &
Management GmbH, Stuttgart

Technisch-wirtschaftliches Controlling
DS-Plan GmbH, Stuttgart

Objektüberwachung

**7 Standardhallen, Mittelzone,
Eingang West**
wulf+ass. Architekten GmbH,
Tobias Wulf, Kai Bierich,
Alexander Vohl, Stuttgart

**Hochhalle, Congresscenter mit
Tiefgarage, Eingang Ost**
Gassmann + Grossmann,
Baumanagement GmbH, Stuttgart

Parkhaus
IGS Ingenieur Gemeinschaft Seidel
GmbH, Stuttgart

Fachplaner

Tragwerksplaner Messe
Mayr + Ludescher Beratende
Ingenieure GmbH, Stuttgart
Guido Ludescher

**Tragwerksplaner Parkhaus und äußere
Verkehrserschließung**
Leonhardt, Andrä und
Partner, Stuttgart
Volkhard Angelmaier

**Tragwerksplanung Congresscenter,
Eingänge und Tiefgarage**
Boll und Partner, Stuttgart

Prüfingenieure
Bornscheuer Drexler Eisele GmbH,
Stuttgart, Bernd Friedrich
Bornscheuer
Braschel Control GmbH, Stuttgart,
Reinhold Braschel
Hildenbrand Ingenieure
GmbH + Co. KG, Ludwigsburg,
Peter Hildenbrand
Mayer-Vorfelder und Dinkelacker,
Ingenieurgesellschaft für Bauwesen
GmbH + Co. KG, Sindelfingen,
Hans Jörg Mayer-Vorfelder
Patzak Ingenieurbüro, Stuttgart,
Manfred Patzak
Peter und Lochner, Beratende
Ingenieure für Bauwesen GmbH,
Stuttgart, Dieter Lippold

Informations- und Orientierungssystem
Büro Uebele
Visuelle Kommunikation, Stuttgart
Andreas Uebele, Katrin Dittmann

Infrastrukturplanung
Spiekermann GmbH, Beratende
Ingenieure, Stuttgart

**Geotechnik, Hydrogeologie,
Umwelttechnik**
Smoltczyk & Partner GmbH, Stuttgart

Vermessung
intermetric GmbH, Stuttgart

Äußere Verkehrserschließung
BUNG Ingenieure AG, Stuttgart

**Technische Ausstattung Elektrik,
FA, Baustrom**
ibb Burrer & Deuring Ingenieurbüro
GmbH, Ludwigsburg

Fernmeldetechnik
Ingenieurbüro W. Braun, Stuttgart

Technische Ausstattung HLSK, MSR
Brandi IGH Ingenieure GmbH,
NL Ostfildern

Technische Ausstattung HLSK
Scholze Ingenieurgesellschaft mbH,
Leinfelden-Echterdingen

Technische Ausrüstung MSR
Planungsgruppe M+M AG,
Ingenieurgesellschaft für
Gebäudetechnik, Böblingen

**Technische Ausstattung
Küchen/Gastronomie**
Ingenieurbüro Ködel, Gastronomie
Planung Lebensmittelverfahrens-
technik, Ismaning
K&P Planungsbüro GmbH, Düsseldorf

Verkehrsleitsysteme äußere Messe
Ingenieurbüro Thomas und Partner,
Möglingen

Parkleitsysteme
Schnüll Haller und Partner, Hannover

Fassaden – Beratung und Planung
Erich Mosbacher Planungsbüro für
Fassadentechnik, Friedrichshafen

Bühnentechnik – Beratung und Planung
theater projekte daberto + kollegen
planungsgesellschaft mbh, München

Berater

Bauphysik/Schallschutz
ifb Wolfgang Sorge Ingenieurbüro
für Bauphysik GmbH,
Beratende Ingenieure VBI, Nürnberg

Brandschutz
HHP Nord/Ost Beratende Ingenieure
GmbH, Braunschweig

Lichttechnik
Bartenbach LichtLabor GmbH,
Aldrans/Innsbruck

Boden-/Wassergutachter
Smoltczyk & Partner GmbH, Stuttgart

Nutzerberatung (LMS)
Arnold & Partner Consulting, Zürich

Verkehrsberatung Parkhaus/Tiefgarage
Karajan Ingenieure Beraten + Planen
Ingenieurgesellschaft mbH, Stuttgart

**SiGeKO Sicherheits- und
Gesundheitsschutzkoordination**
Ingenieurbüro Schnitzspahn, Bondorf

Sicherheitstechnik
Geiger Systemberater
Sicherheitstechnik,
Leinfelden-Echterdingen

Ausführende Firmen
Contractors

ARGE Tiefbau
F. Kirchhoff Straßenbau
GmbH & Co. KG, NL Stuttgart,
Leinfelden-Echterdingen
Leonhard Weiss
GmbH & Co. KG, Göppingen
Karl Fischer GmbH & Co. OHG,
Weilheim-Teck

ARGE Straßenbau
Vogel-Bau GmbH, Lahr
Reif Bauunternehmung
GmbH & Co. KG, Baiersbronn

ARGE Heerstraßenbrücke
Max Früh GmbH & Co. KG, Achern
Heberger Bau AG, Schifferstadt
Vogel-Bau GmbH, Lahr
Reif Bauunternehmung
GmbH & Co. KG, Baiersbronn

ARGE Rohbau
Max Bögl Bauunternehmung
GmbH & Co. KG, Stuttgart
Leonhard Weiss
GmbH & Co. KG, Göppingen

ARGE Parkhaus
Wayss & Freytag
Ingenieurbau AG, Stuttgart
Baresel GmbH,
Leinfelden-Echterdingen
Donges Stahlbau GmbH, Darmstadt

ARGE TK-Linien
Hermann Stumpp
GmbH & Co. KG, Stuttgart
RMS Richard Mayer
GmbH & Co. KG, Sindelfingen
Gottlob Brodbeck
GmbH & Co. KG, Metzingen

ARGE Elektrotechnik
Imtech Deutschland
GmbH & Co. KG, Stuttgart
Schlagenhauf, Ellwangen
Speidel GmbH & Co. KG, Göppingen
Siemens Building Technologies
GmbH & Co. oHG, Stuttgart

ARGE Datentechnik
Imtech ICT Deutschland GmbH, Aalen

INES
T-Systems Business Service GmbH,
Mühlheim a.d. Ruhr
Scheidt & Bachmann GmbH,
Mönchengladbach
Klaus Gindl GmbH, Rheinstetten
dimedis GmbH, Köln

Fernmeldetechnik
PKE Elektronics AG, Wien
PKE Deutschland GmbH, Stuttgart

Mobilfunk
Vivento Technical Services
GmbH, Rastatt

Blitzschutz
Fautz & Partner Blitzschutzbau,
Villingendorf
Ludwigs Blitzschutz-Erdungsanlagen
GmbH & Co. KG, Krefeld

Gebäudeautomation
Neuberger Gebäudeautomaten
GmbH & Co. KG, Rothenburg

Sanitärinstallationen
Schwender KG, Thurnau
Helmut Herbert
GmbH & Co., Einhausen
RGT Rhönland Gesundheitstechnik
GmbH & Co. KG, Bad Neustadt
Heima GmbH & Co. KG, Lichtenstein

Heizung, Klima, Lüftung
M+W Zander Gebäudetechnik
GmbH, Stuttgart
Imtech Deutschland
GmbH & Co. KG, Stuttgart
Siegle+Epple
GmbH & Co. KG, Stuttgart
AXIMA GmbH Region Württemberg,
Stuttgart
Stangl GmbH, Deggendorf
Pleitz GmbH, Laucha

Sprinkleranlagen
Kraftanlagen Heidelberg GmbH,
Heidelberg
AXIMA GmbH Region
Württemberg, Stuttgart

Küchentechnik
Hörstke Großkücheneinrichtungen
GmbH, Witten
Winterhalter Gastronom GmbH,
Meckenbeuren
Kälte Eckert GmbH, Markgröningen
Winkler Design
GmbH & Co., Röttingen

Bühnentechnik, Beleuchtung,
Medientechnik
W+P Anlagenbau GmbH,
Weiherhammer
Zeiler-Technik,
Neuötting-Eisenfelden
Thomann Audio Professionell,
Burgebrach

Schlosserarbeiten
A.I.S. Stahlbau GmbH, Willich
Stahlbau Nägele GmbH, Eislingen
Oschwald GmbH, Meßkirch

Stahlbauarbeiten
Donges Stahlbau GmbH, Darmstadt
Perr Stahlbau Betriebs GmbH,
Dietfurt
Krupp Stahlbau Hannover (KSH)
GmbH, nachmals
Eiffel Deutschland
Stahltechnologie GmbH
Haslinger Stahlbau GmbH,
A-9560 Feldkirchen
Stahlbau Behrens
GmbH & Co. KG, Vahldorf

Fassadenbauarbeiten
Gebr. Schneider GmbH & Co. KG
Fensterfabrik Fassadenbau,
Stimpfach
Roschmann Konstruktionen aus
Stahl und Glas GmbH, Gersthofen
Kulkwitzer Stahl- und Metallbau
GmbH & Co. KG,
04420 Markranstädt

Innenfassaden
Seufert-Niklaus GmbH, Bastheim
K. Westermann GmbH & Co. KG,
Denkendorf
Trauschke Brandschutz GmbH,
Appenweier

Aufzugsanlagen, Fahrtreppen
Rangger Aufzüge GmbH/DAT
Deutsche Aufzugs-Technik, Berlin
OTIS GmbH & Co. KG, Fellbach
Schindler Aufzüge und Fahrtreppen
GmbH, Frankfurt/Main

Dächer Montage, Verglasung, Abdichtung
Fritz Technologie GmbH, Murr
Jet Brakel Aero GmbH, Voerda
Göbel Dach GmbH, Blumberg
R. Schweiger KG, Gräfeling

Stahltüren, Toranlagen
Jansen Brandschutz-Tore,
Kirchheim/Teck

Estricharbeiten
G. Theodor Freese GmbH, Bremen
SPOMA Parkett und Ausbau GmbH,
Magdeburg

Betonwerksteinarbeiten
Gustav Popp GmbH & Co. KG,
Norderstedt

Fliesenarbeiten
Fliesenverlegung von Au, Harrer,
Fliesen Gehrung GmbH, Nürtingen

Putz- und Stuckarbeiten
ER-PA Bau Ayhan Erdogan, Berlin

Parkettarbeiten
Artimento GmbH & Co. KG,
Magdeburg

Bodenbelagsarbeiten
Raumstudio Falter GmbH & Co.,
Fellbach
Aktürk Fussbodentechnik, Darmstadt

Systemtrennwände,
mobile Trennwände, WC-Trennwände
Strähle Raum-Systeme GmbH,
Waiblingen
Kirchner Goldbeck GmbH,
Frankfurt/Main
Kemmlit-Bauelemente GmbH,
Dußlingen

Trockenbauarbeiten
Baierl & Demmelhuber
Innenausbau GmbH, Töging am Inn
Rossaro Gipsbau
GmbH & Co. KG, Aalen
Manfred Lück GmbH, Backnang

Metalldecken
Schmid GmbH, Simmerberg/Allgäu
Jaeger Akustik GmbH & Co. KG
Leipzig, Zwenkau

Malerarbeiten
Bernhard Weber GmbH, Stuttgart
Bilfinger Berger AG, Stuttgart
B & B Profi Lehmann, Windischleuba

Schreinerarbeiten
K. Westermann GmbH & Co. KG,
Denkendorf
Albert Stegmüller Innenausbau
GmbH, Rosenfeld
Lindner AG, Arnstorf

Orientierungssysteme
Signature Deutschland GmbH,
Birkenfeld
Kaufmann Ulm Lichtwerbung GmbH,
Neu-Ulm
Schreiner Coburg GmbH, Coburg

Schließanlage
Weckbacher GmbH, Dortmund

Messepark, Außenanlagen
Mabau GmbH, Ravensburg
Jörg Seidenspinner Garten- und
Landschaftsbau GmbH, Stuttgart
Stier Gartenbau
GmbH & Co. KG, Stuttgart
Toriello GmbH Landschaftspflege,
Nagold

Autoren

Ulrich Bauer
Dipl.-Ing. (arch.), geboren 1939 in Schwä-bisch-Hall, studierte nach einer Maurer- und Zimmererlehre Architektur an der TU München und absolvierte 1970 die Zweite Große Staatsprüfung im höheren technischen Verwaltungsdienst des Landes Nordrhein-Westfalen. Anschließend arbeitete er als Bauassessor und Leiter des Planungsamtes in Troisdorf und wurde dort 1973 Beigeordneter. 1983 wurde er zum Baubürgermeister der Stadt Heilbronn bestellt und war 1990 bis 1998 Oberbürgermeister der Stadt Esslingen am Neckar. Seit Oktober 1998 ist er Geschäftsführer der Projektgesellschaft Neue Messe GmbH & Co. KG.

Falk Jaeger
Prof. Dr.-Ing., geboren 1950 in Ottweiler/ Saar, studierte in Braunschweig, Stuttgart und Tübingen Architektur und Kunstgeschichte und wurde an der TU Hannover promoviert. Seit 1976 arbeitet er als freier Architekturkritiker. 1983–1988 war er Assistent am Institut für Baugeschichte und Bauaufnahme der TU Berlin, hatte Lehraufträge an verschiedenen Hochschulen und war 1993 bis 2000 Dozent und apl. Professor für Architekturtheorie an der TU Dresden. Er lebt als freier Publizist, Kurator und Fachjournalist für Rundfunk, Tages- und Fachpresse in Berlin.

Michael Ohnewald
geboren 1964 in Stuttgart, studierte Kommunikationswissenschaften in Berlin und wurde Journalist. Er arbeitet seit 1995 bei der Stuttgarter Zeitung und ist dort als leitender Redakteur für Reportagen aus der Region Stuttgart zuständig. Für seine Reportagen und Porträts wurde er mehrfach ausgezeichnet, unter anderem mit dem Theodor-Wolff-Preis, dem renommiertesten Journalistenpreis in Deutschland, mit dem Konrad-Adenauer-Preis und mit dem Wächterpreis der deutschen Tagespresse.

Tobias Wulf
Prof. Dipl.-Ing. (arch.), geboren 1956 in Frankfurt am Main, studierte an der Universität Stuttgart, arbeitete bei Auer und Weber (Stuttgart), Joachim Schürmann (Köln) und Gottfried Böhm (Köln) und gründete 1987 sein eigenes Büro in Stuttgart. Seit 1996 besteht die Partnerschaft Wulf & Partner. 1987–1991 hatte er einen Lehrauftrag für Entwerfen an der Universität Stuttgart, seit 1991 ist er Professor für Baukonstruktion und Entwerfen an der FHT Stuttgart.

Kai Bierich
Prof. Dipl.-Ing. (arch.), geboren 1957 in Hamburg, studierte an der TH Darmstadt und arbeitete bei Behnisch & Partner sowie seit 1992 bei Tobias Wulf, mit dem er 1996 in Partnerschaft trat. 1989–1996 hatte er einen Lehrauftrag für Entwerfen an der Universität Stuttgart, war 1996 –1999 Dozent an der Staatlichen Akademie der Bildenden Künste in Stuttgart und ist seit 2006 Gastprofessor an der Universität Nankai, China.

Alexander Vohl
Dipl.-Ing. (arch.), geboren 1961 in Stuttgart, studierte an der Freien Kunstschule Stuttgart, an der TH Darmstadt und an der Universität Stuttgart. Er arbeitete bei Behnisch & Partner und ab 1991 bei Tobias Wulf, mit dem er 1996 in Partnerschaft trat. Er hat einen Lehrauftrag für Entwerfen an der Universität Stuttgart.

Authors

Ulrich Bauer
Dipl.-Ing. (arch.), was born in Schwäbisch-Hall in 1939. After an apprenticeship as a bricklayer and carpenter, he studied architecture at the Technical University of Munich and, in 1970, completed the Zweite Große Staatsprüfung im höheren technischen Verwaltungsdienst (Second examination for the higher-level technical civil service) of the state of North Rhine Westphalia. He then worked as a building assessor and head of the planning office in Troisdorf, where he became a councillor in 1973. In 1983, he was appointed as the »building mayor« of the city of Heilbronn and, 1990 to 1998, was lord mayor of Esslingen am Neckar. Since October 1998, he has been managing director of Projektgesellschaft Neue Messe GmbH & Co. KG.

Falk Jaeger
Prof. Dr.-Ing., born in Ottweiler/Saar in 1950, studied architecture and the history of art in Braunschweig, Stuttgart and Tübingen, later obtaining his doctorate at the Technical University of Hanover. From 1976, he worked as a freelance architecture critic. From 1982 to 1988, he was an assistant at the Institut für Baugeschichte und Bauaufnahme (institute for architectural history and records) of the Technical University of Berlin, worked as a lecturer at various institutes of higher education and, from 1993 to 2000, was lecturer and professor for architectural theory at the Technical University of Dresden. He now works as a freelance writer, curator and specialist journalist for radio, newspapers and the trade press in Berlin.

Michael Ohnewald
Born in Stuttgart in 1964, he studied communication sciences in Berlin and became a journalist. Since 1995, he has worked for the newspaper »Stuttgarter Zeitung«, where he is the editor in chief, responsible for reporting from the Stuttgart region. He has received several awards for his reports and portraits, including the Theodor Wolff Prize (the best-known prize for journalism in Germany), the Konrad Adenauer Prize and the Wächterpreis (prize for courageous reporting) of the German daily press.

Tobias Wulf
Prof. Dipl.-Ing. (arch.), born in Frankfurt am Main in 1956, studied at Stuttgart university, worked for Auer und Weber (Stuttgart), Joachim Schürmann (Cologne) and Gottfried Böhm (Cologne). In 1987, he established his own office in Stuttgart. The partnership, Wulf & Partner, has existed since 1996. From 1987 to 1991, he taught design at Stuttgart university and, since 1991, he has been professor for building construction and design at Stuttgart technical college.

Kai Bierich
Prof. Dipl.-Ing. (arch.), born in Hamburg in 1957, studied at the Technical University of Darmstadt and worked for Behnisch & Partner and, since 1992, for Tobias Wulf, with whom he entered into a partnership in 1996. From 1989 to 1996, he taught design at Stuttgart university. From 1996 to 1999, he was a lecturer at the Staatliche Akademie der Bildenden Künste (state academy of fine arts) in Stuttgart. Since 2006, he has been a visiting professor at Nankai university in China.

Alexander Vohl
Dipl.-Ing. (arch.), born in Stuttgart in 1961, studied at the Freie Kunstschule (free school of art) Stuttgart, at the Technical University of Darmstadt and at Stuttgart university. He worked for Behnisch & Partner and, from 1991, for Tobias Wulf, with whom he entered into a partnership in 1996. He teaches design at Stuttgart university.

Dank

Um das Projekt der neuen Landesmesse Stuttgart haben sich viele Beteiligte Verdienste erworben. Großer Dank gilt insbesondere den Gesellschaftern der Projektgesellschaft Neue Messe, dem Land Baden-Württemberg, dem früheren Ministerpräsidenten Erwin Teufel und Ministerpräsident Günther H. Oettinger; der Landeshauptstadt Stuttgart mit Oberbürgermeister Dr. Wolfgang Schuster; dem Verband Region Stuttgart mit Regionaldirektor Dr. Bernd Steinacher sowie dem atypisch stillen Gesellschafter Flughafen Stuttgart GmbH mit seinen Geschäftsführern Professor Georg Fundel und Walter Schoefer.

Mein Dank gilt ferner dem Aufsichtsrat, der unter dem kontinuierlichen Vorsitz von Herrn Staatssekretär a.D. Dr. Horst Mehrländer seit Mai 1998 in 68 Sitzungen die wesentlichen Entscheidungen getroffen hat.

Anerkennung und Dank gilt den Architekten Professor Tobias Wulf, Professor Kai Bierich und Alexander Vohl, die mit ihrem engagierten Team großartige Architektur und ein wunderbar leichtes Bauwerk geschaffen haben, das sich trotz riesiger Mengen an Stahl, Beton und Glas geschickt und harmonisch in die Filderlandschaft einfügt.

Die Messe wäre nie gebaut worden ohne die hervorragende Beratung durch Rechtsanwalt Professor Dr. Klaus-Peter Dolde und seine Partner, der uns auf allen Gerichtsebenen bravourös vertrat und uns letztendlich zur uneingeschränkten Baugenehmigung verhalf.

Ferner ist dem Verfahrensmanager Dr. Thomas Seeliger, der das Planfeststellungsverfahren professionell begleitet hat, zu danken.

Ohne den großen Einsatz der Projektsteuerer von Drees & Sommer unter der Leitung von Thomas Jaißle und Uwe Tyralla wäre dieses riesige Projekt nicht zu schultern gewesen. Sie standen der Projektgesellschaft mit ihrer großen Erfahrung und ihrem Wissen ständig zur Seite und garantierten so die termingerechte Fertigstellung im Kostenrahmen.

Zu danken ist ferner den zahlreichen Fachingenieuren, Bauleitern und Beratern, die unermüdlich dafür sorgten, dass die Baustelle funktionierte, sowie allen am Bau beteiligten Firmen, die mit tausenden von Arbeitern zum Gelingen des großen Werkes beigetragen haben.

Ganz besonders herzlich danke ich – auch im Namen meiner Geschäftsführerkollegen Ulrich Kromer von Baerle und Walter Schoefer – meinen Mitarbeitern, den tüchtigen Damen und Herren der Projektgesellschaft Neue Messe GmbH & Co.KG, die mit kleinem Team bis zur Grenze der Belastbarkeit gingen. Sie haben trotz vieler Widrigkeiten immer an die Realisierung geglaubt und haben es mit höchstem persönlichen Einsatz geschafft, alle Fäden zusammenzuführen, um dieses vorbildliche Projekt fertig zu stellen.

Ulrich Bauer

Many people contributed to the new Stuttgart Trade Fair Centre project. Special thanks go to the partners in the project company Neue Messe, the state of Baden-Württemberg, the former minister president Erwin Teufel, and the current minister president Günther H. Oettinger; to Stuttgart, the state capital with its lord mayor, Dr. Wolfgang Schuster; to the Verband Region Stuttgart with regional director Dr. Bernd Steinacher as well as to the atypically silent partner, Flughafen Stuttgart GmbH, with its directors Professor Georg Fundel and Walter Schoefer.

I would also like to thank the supervisory board which made the important decisions in 68 sessions from May 1998 onwards under the continuous chairmanship of State Secretary (retired) Dr. Horst Mehrländer.

A word of appreciation and thanks also goes to the architects, Professor Tobias Wulf, Professor Kai Bierich and Alexander Vohl, who, together with their dedicated team, created a piece of outstanding architecture and a wonderfully lightweight construction which fits succinctly and harmoniously into the landscape in the Filder area, in spite of the huge amounts of steel, concrete and glass.

The trade fair centre would never have been built had it not been for the excellent consulting service provided by lawyer Professor Dr. Klaus-Peter Dolde and his partners who successfully represented us before all the courts and finally helped us to obtain an unrestricted building permit.

We would also like to thank Dr. Thomas Seeliger, who provided professional assistance in all stages of the planning approval procedure.

Without the great commitment of the project controllers from Drees & Sommer, headed by Thomas Jaißle and Uwe Tyralla, it would have been impossible to cope with such an enormous project. They supported the project company with their extensive experience and specialist knowledge, thus guaranteeing that the project was completed on time and within the budget.

We would also like to express our gratitude to the many engineers, construction supervisors and consultants, whose tireless efforts ensured that the activities on the construction site proceeded smoothly, as well as to all the companies who were involved in construction and whose thousands of employees helped to make the project such a success.

On behalf of my fellow directors Ulrich Kromer von Baerle and Walter Schoefer, and also on my own behalf, I must also give special thanks to my employees, the untiring workforce of Projektgesellschaft Neue Messe GmbH & Co.KG, whose small team worked almost to the limits of human capacity. In spite of all the hurdles, they always believed in the task they had been set and, with great personnel effort, managed to join all the threads together in order to complete this model project.

Ulrich Bauer

Bildnachweis
Picture credits

© Roland Halbe, Stuttgart
Umschlagabbildung / Cover photo
Seiten / Pages
002
008–017
086
090–103
106–117
120–125
128–137
196
198
200

© Joachim Siener, Stuttgart
Württembergische Landesbibliothek
Seiten / Pages
018
023 (Abb. / Fig. 01)

© Archiv Jörg Kurz, Stuttgart
Seiten / Pages
023 (Abb. / Fig. 02–05)
024 (Abb. / Fig. 01–03)

© Landesmesse Stuttgart GmbH
Seiten / Pages
027 (Abb. / Fig. 01–05)
028 (Abb. / Fig. 01)

© Jörg Kurz, Stuttgart
Seiten / Pages
028 (Abb. / Fig. 02–05)
031 (Abb. / Fig. 01–04)

© Dieterich Werner, Stuttgart
Seiten / Pages
032
037 (Abb. / Fig. 01–05)

© Horst Rudel, Stuttgart
Seiten / Pages
040
045
046

© Arnim Kilgus, Leinfelden-Echterdingen
Seiten / Pages
058
063 (Abb. / Fig. 01–04)
064–067
068 (Abb. / Fig. 01–04)
070–073
075 (Abb. / Fig. 01–04)
076–077
078 (Abb. / Fig. 01–04)
080
160
163 (Abb. / Fig. 03)
164–165
166 (Abb. / Fig. 01–04)
168–169
171 (Abb. / Fig. 03, 04)
172–173
174 (Abb. / Fig. 01–04)
176

© AG.L.N. Landschaftsplanung und
Naturschutzmanagement, Blaubeuren
Pläne / Plans
Seiten / Pages
182
185
187
189

© Büro Uebele, Stuttgart
Illustrationen / Illustrations
Seiten / Pages
190
193
194
197
199

© Drees & Sommer AG, Stuttgart
Illustrationen / Illustrations
Seite / Page
180

© Mayr + Ludescher
Beratende Ingenieure GmbH, Stuttgart
Seiten / Pages
163 (Abb. / Fig. 01, 02)
171 (Abb. / Fig. 01, 02)

© wulf & partner
Freie Architekten BDA, Stuttgart
Skizzen / Sketches
Seiten / Pages
050
055

Pläne / Plans
Seiten / Pages
138–159